Gender and Power

Understanding the
Dynamics of Influence
and Control

Ernest Brooks

© Copyright 2024 by Ernest Brooks

All Rights Reserved

The presentation of the information is without contract or any type of guarantee assurance. The trademarks that are used are without any consent, and the publication of the trademark is without permission or backing by the trademark owner. All trademarks and brands within this book are for clarifying purposes only and are the owned by the owners themselves, not affiliated with this document.

Table of Contents

Chapter 1

Introduction to Gender and Power

Defining Gender and Power

Gender and power are two fundamental constructs that shape the fabric of human society. They are intricately woven into the social, political, and economic structures that govern our lives. Understanding these concepts requires a nuanced exploration of their definitions, implications, and the ways they intersect to influence individual and collective experiences.

Gender, at its core, refers to the roles, behaviors, activities, and attributes that a given society considers appropriate for men and women. It is a social construct that extends beyond biological differences, encompassing the expectations and norms that dictate how individuals should think, act, and interact based on their perceived sex. Gender is not a static or universal concept; it varies across cultures and historical periods, reflecting the dynamic nature of human societies. It is important to recognize that gender is not binary but exists on a spectrum, allowing for a diverse range of identities and expressions.

Power, on the other hand, is the ability to influence or control the behavior of others, the course of events, or the allocation of resources. It manifests in various forms, including political, economic, social, and cultural power. Power can be overt, as seen in formal positions of authority, or covert, as in the subtle ways individuals and groups exert influence through social norms and cultural narratives. Power is often relational, existing within the context of relationships and interactions between individuals and groups.

The intersection of gender and power is a complex and multifaceted phenomenon. Gender roles and expectations often dictate who holds power and how it is exercised. Historically, patriarchal systems have privileged men, granting them greater access to power and resources while marginalizing women and other gender minorities. This imbalance has perpetuated inequalities and shaped societal structures in ways that reinforce male dominance and female subordination.

However, gender and power are not merely about domination and subjugation. They also encompass the potential for resistance, transformation, and empowerment. Throughout history, individuals and groups have challenged traditional gender roles and power dynamics, advocating for equality and justice. These efforts have led to significant social and political changes, including the expansion of women's rights, the recognition of LGBTQ+ identities, and the dismantling of discriminatory practices.

To define gender and power, it is essential to consider the ways they intersect with other social categories, such as race, class, ethnicity, and sexuality. Intersectionality, a concept introduced by Kimberlé Crenshaw, highlights the interconnectedness of social identities and the ways they compound experiences of privilege and oppression. For example, a white woman and a woman of color may both face gender-based discrimination, but their experiences will differ due to the additional layer of racial dynamics. Similarly, a wealthy man and a working-class man may both benefit from male privilege, but their access to power will be influenced by their economic status.

Understanding gender and power also requires an examination of the cultural narratives and ideologies that shape our perceptions and behaviors. Media, literature, religion, and education play significant roles in constructing and perpetuating gender norms and power relations. These cultural artifacts often reflect and reinforce dominant ideologies, but they can also serve as sites of resistance and transformation. By critically engaging with these narratives, individuals can challenge and redefine the meanings of gender and power in their own lives and communities.

In contemporary society, the definitions of gender and power are continually evolving. The rise of social movements, such as feminism, LGBTQ+ rights, and Black Lives Matter, has brought increased attention to issues of gender and power, prompting critical discussions and debates. These movements have highlighted the need for more inclusive and equitable approaches to understanding and addressing power dynamics. They have also emphasized the importance of recognizing and valuing diverse gender identities and expressions.

As we navigate the complexities of gender and power, it is crucial to adopt a critical and reflective approach. This involves questioning assumptions, challenging stereotypes, and embracing diversity. It also requires a commitment to social justice and the pursuit of equality for all individuals, regardless of their gender identity or expression. By doing so, we can work towards a more inclusive and equitable society where power is shared and gender is celebrated in all its diversity.

Historical Context of Gender Roles

The tapestry of human history is rich with the threads of gender roles, intricately woven into the social, economic, and political fabric of societies across the globe. To understand the historical context of gender roles, one must delve into the evolution of these roles over time, examining how they have been shaped by cultural, religious, and economic forces. This exploration reveals not only the persistence of certain gender norms but also the dynamic shifts that have occurred in response to changing societal needs and values.

In ancient civilizations, gender roles were often dictated by the demands of survival and the division of labor necessary for community sustenance. In hunter-gatherer societies, men typically assumed the role of hunters, while women gathered food and cared for children. This division was not merely a reflection of physical capabilities but also a strategic allocation of resources to ensure the group's survival. As societies transitioned to agrarian economies, the roles of men and women began to shift. Men took on the labor-intensive tasks of farming and animal husbandry, while women managed the household and contributed to agricultural production in various capacities.

The rise of organized religions further entrenched gender roles, often codifying them into religious texts and doctrines. In many cultures, religious institutions became powerful arbiters of social norms, prescribing distinct roles for men and women. For instance, in ancient Greece, women were largely confined to the domestic sphere, their roles defined by their relationships to men as daughters, wives, and mothers. Similarly, in medieval Europe, the Christian Church played a significant role in shaping gender roles, emphasizing the virtues of chastity, obedience, and piety for women, while men were encouraged to pursue leadership and authority.

The advent of the industrial revolution marked a significant turning point in the history of gender roles. As economies shifted from agrarian to industrial, the demand for labor in factories and urban centers drew men away from rural areas, altering traditional family structures. Women, too, began to enter the workforce, albeit in limited and often exploitative conditions. This period saw the emergence of the "separate spheres" ideology, which posited that men and women occupied distinct domains: men in the public sphere of work and politics, and women in the private sphere of home and family. This ideology reinforced the notion of male breadwinners and female homemakers, a concept that persisted well into the 20th century.

The 19th and 20th centuries witnessed significant challenges to traditional gender roles, driven by social, political, and economic changes. The suffrage movement, which gained momentum in the late 19th century, was a pivotal force in advocating for women's rights and challenging the notion of female subservience. Women across the world organized, protested, and lobbied for the right to vote, ultimately achieving suffrage in many countries. This victory was not merely a political milestone but also a catalyst for broader social change, as women began to assert their rights in other areas, including education, employment, and reproductive autonomy.

World Wars I and II further disrupted traditional gender roles, as women were called upon to fill roles traditionally occupied by men who had gone to fight. Women worked in factories, served in auxiliary military units, and took on leadership roles in their communities. These experiences challenged prevailing notions of gender capabilities and laid the groundwork for the feminist movements of the mid-20th century. The post-war period saw a renewed emphasis on domesticity, particularly in Western societies, as men returned from war and women were encouraged to relinquish their wartime roles. However, the seeds of change had been sown, and the feminist movements of the 1960s and 1970s built upon this legacy, advocating for gender equality and challenging the patriarchal structures that had long defined gender roles.

The feminist movements of the 20th century were diverse and multifaceted, encompassing a range of ideologies and strategies. The first wave of feminism focused primarily on legal issues, such as suffrage and property rights, while the second wave addressed broader social and cultural inequalities, including workplace discrimination, reproductive rights, and sexual liberation. The third wave, emerging in the late 20th century, emphasized intersectionality and the need to address the diverse experiences of women across race, class, and sexuality. These movements have had a profound impact on gender roles, challenging traditional norms and advocating for greater equality and representation.

Despite these advances, gender roles continue to be a site of contestation and negotiation. In many parts of the world, traditional gender norms persist, often reinforced by cultural, religious, and economic factors. In some societies, women continue to face significant barriers to education, employment, and political participation, while men may be constrained by rigid expectations of masculinity. The struggle for gender equality is ongoing, requiring continued advocacy, education, and policy change.

The Intersection of Gender and Authority

Authority, a concept deeply embedded in the structures of society, often intersects with gender in ways that shape individual experiences and societal norms. This intersection is not merely a matter of who holds power, but also how power is perceived, exercised, and challenged across different gender identities. Understanding this dynamic requires an exploration of the historical, cultural, and social contexts that have influenced the distribution and exercise of authority.

Throughout history, authority has often been synonymous with masculinity. Patriarchal systems have traditionally positioned men as the primary holders of power, both in public and private spheres. This has been evident in political leadership, religious institutions, and familial structures, where male authority figures have dominated decision-making processes. The association of authority with masculinity has perpetuated stereotypes that equate leadership qualities with traits traditionally ascribed to men, such as assertiveness, rationality, and strength.

However, the intersection of gender and authority is not solely about male dominance. Women and gender minorities have historically exercised authority in various forms, often in ways that challenge traditional power structures. In many cultures, women have held significant influence within their communities, whether as matriarchs, spiritual leaders, or healers. These roles, while sometimes overlooked in historical narratives, demonstrate the diverse ways in which authority can be manifested and recognized.

The modern era has seen significant shifts in the intersection of gender and authority, driven by social movements advocating for gender equality and representation. The feminist movements of the 20th and 21st centuries have been instrumental in challenging the traditional association of authority with masculinity. By advocating for women's rights and representation in leadership positions, these movements have sought to redefine authority in more inclusive and equitable terms.

One of the key challenges in addressing the intersection of gender and authority is the persistence of gender biases and stereotypes. These biases often manifest in the form of double standards, where behaviors deemed authoritative in men are perceived as aggressive or inappropriate in women. This can create barriers for women and gender minorities seeking to exercise authority, whether in the workplace, politics, or other areas of public life. Addressing these biases requires a critical examination of the cultural narratives that shape our perceptions of authority and gender.

The intersection of gender and authority is also influenced by intersectionality, a concept that highlights the interconnectedness of social identities and the ways they compound experiences of privilege and oppression. For example, a woman of color may face unique challenges in exercising authority due to the combined effects of gender and racial biases. Similarly, LGBTQ+ individuals may encounter additional barriers in asserting authority due to societal prejudices related to sexual orientation or gender identity. Recognizing these intersecting identities is crucial for understanding the complexities of authority and for promoting more inclusive approaches to leadership.

In recent years, there has been a growing recognition of the need for diverse leadership styles that reflect a broader range of gender identities and expressions. This has led to a reevaluation of traditional leadership models and the exploration of alternative approaches that prioritize collaboration, empathy, and inclusivity. By embracing diverse perspectives and experiences, organizations and institutions can foster environments where authority is shared and exercised in ways that reflect the values and needs of all members.

The intersection of gender and authority also extends to the realm of policy and governance. Gender-responsive policies that address the specific needs and challenges faced by women and gender minorities are essential for promoting equality and empowerment. This includes policies related to reproductive rights, workplace equality, and protection against gender-based violence. By incorporating gender perspectives into policy-making processes, governments and organizations can create more equitable and just societies.

Education plays a critical role in shaping the intersection of gender and authority. By challenging traditional gender norms and promoting diverse role models, educational institutions can empower individuals to exercise authority in ways that reflect their unique identities and experiences. This includes providing opportunities for leadership development and fostering environments where diverse voices are heard and valued.

Power Structures in Society

Power structures in society are the invisible frameworks that dictate how authority, influence, and resources are distributed among individuals and groups. These structures are deeply embedded in the social, political, and economic systems that govern our lives, shaping our interactions and opportunities.

Understanding these power structures requires a critical examination of the historical, cultural, and institutional forces that have shaped them, as well as the ways they continue to evolve and impact our world.

At the heart of power structures lies the concept of hierarchy, a system of ranking individuals or groups based on perceived authority, status, or importance. Hierarchies are prevalent in various aspects of society, from government and business to education and family. They often reflect and reinforce existing social norms and values, dictating who holds power and how it is exercised. In many cases, hierarchies are maintained through formal institutions, such as laws, policies, and organizational structures, which legitimize and perpetuate power imbalances.

One of the most pervasive power structures in society is the patriarchy, a system in which men hold primary power and dominate roles of political leadership, moral authority, and control over property. Patriarchy has historically marginalized women and gender minorities, limiting their access to resources and opportunities. This power structure is reinforced through cultural narratives and social norms that prioritize male authority and privilege, often at the expense of gender equality.

Economic systems also play a significant role in shaping power structures. Capitalism, for example, is characterized by the concentration of wealth and resources in the hands of a few, creating significant disparities in power and influence. This economic power is often intertwined with political power, as wealthy individuals and corporations exert influence over policy-making processes and government decisions. The resulting power imbalances can perpetuate social inequalities, limiting access to education, healthcare, and other essential services for marginalized communities.

Political power structures are another critical component of societal hierarchies. Governments and political institutions wield significant authority over the lives of individuals, shaping policies and laws that impact everything from civil rights to economic opportunities. In many cases, political power is concentrated in the hands of a few, leading to systems of governance that prioritize the interests of the elite over those of the general population. This concentration of power can result in corruption, lack of accountability, and the erosion of democratic principles.

Cultural power structures are equally influential in shaping societal norms and values. Media, religion, and education are powerful tools for disseminating cultural narratives and reinforcing social hierarchies. These institutions often reflect and perpetuate dominant ideologies, shaping our perceptions of gender, race, class, and other social categories. By controlling the flow of information and shaping public discourse, cultural power structures can influence individual beliefs and behaviors, reinforcing existing power dynamics.

Despite the persistence of these power structures, they are not immutable. Throughout history, individuals and groups have challenged and resisted oppressive power structures, advocating for social change and justice. Social movements, such as the civil rights movement, feminist movements, and LGBTQ+ rights movements, have been instrumental in challenging existing power dynamics and advocating for equality and representation. These movements have highlighted the need for more inclusive and equitable power structures that reflect the diversity and complexity of human experiences.

One of the key challenges in addressing power structures is the need for systemic change. This requires a critical examination of the institutions and practices that perpetuate power imbalances, as well as the development of alternative models that prioritize equity and justice. For example, efforts to address economic inequality may involve advocating for progressive taxation, living wages, and access to affordable healthcare and education. Similarly, efforts to promote gender equality may involve challenging patriarchal norms and advocating for policies that support women's rights and representation.

Education plays a crucial role in challenging power structures and promoting social change. By fostering critical thinking and encouraging individuals to question existing norms and values, education can empower individuals to challenge oppressive power dynamics and advocate for more equitable systems. This includes promoting diverse perspectives and experiences, as well as providing opportunities for marginalized communities to have their voices heard and valued.

The role of technology in shaping power structures is also increasingly significant. The rise of digital platforms and social media has transformed the ways in which information is disseminated and consumed,

creating new opportunities for individuals and groups
to challenge existing power dynamics. However,
technology can also reinforce existing power
structures, as seen in issues related to data privacy,
surveillance, and the concentration of power in the
hands of tech giants. Navigating the complexities of
technology and power requires a critical examination
of the ways in which digital tools can be used to
promote equity and justice.

The Importance of Understanding Gender Dynamics

Gender dynamics are the subtle and overt ways in
which gender influences interactions, relationships,
and power structures within society. Understanding
these dynamics is crucial for fostering environments
that are equitable, inclusive, and respectful of all
individuals, regardless of their gender identity. By
examining the ways in which gender shapes our
experiences and interactions, we can begin to
dismantle the barriers that perpetuate inequality and
create spaces where everyone can thrive.

At the core of gender dynamics is the recognition that
gender is not merely a binary classification of male
and female, but a complex spectrum of identities and
expressions. This understanding challenges
traditional notions of gender roles and expectations,
which have historically dictated how individuals
should behave based on their perceived sex. By
acknowledging the diversity of gender identities, we
can create more inclusive environments that respect
and celebrate individual differences.

One of the key reasons for understanding gender dynamics is the impact they have on power relations. Gender often intersects with other social categories, such as race, class, and sexuality, to create unique experiences of privilege and oppression. For example, a white woman and a woman of color may both face gender-based discrimination, but their experiences will differ due to the additional layer of racial dynamics. Similarly, a wealthy man and a working-class man may both benefit from male privilege, but their access to power will be influenced by their economic status. Recognizing these intersecting identities is essential for addressing the complexities of power dynamics and promoting equity and justice.

Gender dynamics also play a significant role in shaping workplace environments. Gender disparities in leadership, the gender pay gap, and workplace harassment are all manifestations of gender dynamics that can create barriers to equality and empowerment. By understanding these dynamics, organizations can implement strategies to promote gender equity, such as mentorship programs, diversity training, and policies that support work-life balance. Creating inclusive workplaces not only benefits individuals but also enhances organizational performance by fostering diverse perspectives and innovation.

In educational settings, understanding gender dynamics is crucial for creating inclusive learning environments that support the success of all students. Gender biases and stereotypes can influence educational experiences and outcomes, affecting everything from classroom interactions to career aspirations. By challenging these biases and promoting diverse role models, educators can empower students to pursue their interests and talents, regardless of gender. This includes providing opportunities for leadership development and encouraging students to question traditional gender norms and expectations.

The media also plays a significant role in shaping gender dynamics by influencing public perceptions and attitudes. Representation of gender in media can reinforce or challenge stereotypes, shaping how individuals view themselves and others. By critically engaging with media content and advocating for diverse and accurate representations of gender, individuals can challenge harmful narratives and promote more inclusive and equitable portrayals. This includes supporting media that highlights the experiences and contributions of marginalized communities and advocating for greater diversity in media industries.

Understanding gender dynamics is also essential for fostering healthy and equitable relationships. Power imbalances in romantic relationships, family structures, and friendships can create dynamics that are harmful and oppressive. By recognizing and addressing these imbalances, individuals can build relationships that are based on mutual respect, communication, and equality. This includes challenging traditional gender roles and expectations, promoting open and honest communication, and supporting each other's autonomy and agency.

In the realm of politics and governance, understanding gender dynamics is crucial for promoting policies and practices that support gender equality and representation. Women and gender minorities have historically been underrepresented in political leadership, limiting their influence on policy-making processes. By advocating for gender-responsive policies and supporting diverse candidates, individuals can promote more inclusive and equitable governance. This includes addressing issues such as reproductive rights, gender-based violence, and access to education and healthcare.

Chapter 2

Historical Perspectives on Gender and Power

Gender Roles Through the Ages

The evolution of gender roles through the ages is a fascinating journey that reflects the changing landscapes of human society. From the earliest hunter-gatherer communities to the complexities of modern life, gender roles have been shaped by a myriad of factors, including economic needs, cultural beliefs, and technological advancements. This historical perspective not only highlights the fluidity of gender roles but also underscores the resilience and adaptability of human societies in the face of change.

In the earliest human societies, survival was the primary concern, and gender roles were largely dictated by the practical needs of the community. In hunter-gatherer groups, men typically took on the role of hunters, venturing into the wild to procure food, while women gathered edible plants and cared for children. This division of labor was not rigid but rather a strategic allocation of resources to ensure the survival of the group. Women often participated in hunting, and men in gathering, depending on the needs and circumstances of the community.

As societies transitioned to agriculture, the roles of men and women began to shift. The advent of farming required a more settled lifestyle, leading to the establishment of permanent settlements and the development of complex social structures. Men typically took on the labor-intensive tasks of plowing fields and managing livestock, while women were responsible for domestic duties and food preparation. This division of labor was reinforced by the growing importance of property ownership and inheritance, which often favored male lineage.

The rise of ancient civilizations brought about significant changes in gender roles, as societies became more stratified and hierarchical. In many cultures, patriarchal systems emerged, with men holding positions of power and authority in political, religious, and economic spheres. Women were often relegated to the domestic sphere, their roles defined by their relationships to men as daughters, wives, and mothers. However, this was not universally the case. In ancient Egypt, for example, women could own property, initiate divorce, and even rule as pharaohs, demonstrating the diversity of gender roles across different cultures.

The medieval period saw the entrenchment of gender roles within the framework of feudalism and the influence of religious institutions. In Europe, the Christian Church played a significant role in shaping societal norms, emphasizing the virtues of chastity, obedience, and piety for women. Men were encouraged to pursue leadership and authority, both in the secular and religious realms. Despite these constraints, women found ways to exercise influence, whether through religious vocations, as in the case of abbesses and mystics, or through the management of estates in the absence of their husbands.

The Renaissance and Enlightenment periods brought about a renewed interest in individualism and human potential, challenging traditional notions of gender roles. The rise of humanism emphasized education and intellectual pursuits, leading to increased opportunities for women in the arts and sciences. However, these opportunities were often limited to women of certain social classes, and the prevailing belief in male superiority persisted. The Enlightenment's emphasis on reason and progress laid the groundwork for future challenges to gender inequality, as thinkers began to question the naturalness of gender roles and advocate for women's rights.

The industrial revolution marked a turning point in the history of gender roles, as economic and social changes disrupted traditional family structures. The demand for labor in factories and urban centers drew men away from rural areas, while women began to enter the workforce in greater numbers. This period saw the emergence of the "separate spheres" ideology, which posited that men and women occupied distinct domains: men in the public sphere of work and politics, and women in the private sphere of home and family. This ideology reinforced the notion of male breadwinners and female homemakers, a concept that persisted well into the 20th century.

The 19th and 20th centuries witnessed significant challenges to traditional gender roles, driven by social, political, and economic changes. The suffrage movement, which gained momentum in the late 19th century, was a pivotal force in advocating for women's rights and challenging the notion of female subservience. Women across the world organized, protested, and lobbied for the right to vote, ultimately achieving suffrage in many countries. This victory was not merely a political milestone but also a catalyst for broader social change, as women began to assert their rights in other areas, including education, employment, and reproductive autonomy.

World Wars I and II further disrupted traditional gender roles, as women were called upon to fill roles traditionally occupied by men who had gone to fight. Women worked in factories, served in auxiliary military units, and took on leadership roles in their communities. These experiences challenged prevailing notions of gender capabilities and laid the groundwork for the feminist movements of the mid-20th century. The post-war period saw a renewed emphasis on domesticity, particularly in Western societies, as men returned from war and women were encouraged to relinquish their wartime roles. However, the seeds of change had been sown, and the feminist movements of the 1960s and 1970s built upon this legacy, advocating for gender equality and challenging the patriarchal structures that had long defined gender roles.

The feminist movements of the 20th century were diverse and multifaceted, encompassing a range of ideologies and strategies. The first wave of feminism focused primarily on legal issues, such as suffrage and property rights, while the second wave addressed broader social and cultural inequalities, including workplace discrimination, reproductive rights, and sexual liberation. The third wave, emerging in the late 20th century, emphasized intersectionality and the need to address the diverse experiences of women across race, class, and sexuality. These movements have had a profound impact on gender roles, challenging traditional norms and advocating for greater equality and representation.

In contemporary society, gender roles continue to evolve, influenced by ongoing social movements, technological advancements, and cultural shifts. The rise of digital platforms and social media has transformed the ways in which gender is expressed and perceived, creating new opportunities for individuals to challenge traditional norms and advocate for change. The increasing visibility of LGBTQ+ communities and the recognition of non-binary and gender-fluid identities have further expanded the understanding of gender roles, highlighting the diversity and complexity of human experiences.

Influential Women in History

Throughout history, women have played pivotal roles in shaping societies, cultures, and nations, often overcoming significant barriers to leave indelible marks on the world. Their stories are a testament to resilience, courage, and the relentless pursuit of justice and equality. By examining the lives and contributions of influential women, we gain insight into the diverse ways in which they have challenged norms, broken barriers, and inspired generations.

Cleopatra VII of Egypt, one of the most renowned figures of the ancient world, wielded power with intelligence and charisma. As the last active ruler of the Ptolemaic Kingdom of Egypt, she navigated the complex political landscape of the Roman Empire with strategic alliances and diplomatic acumen. Cleopatra's reign was marked by her efforts to restore Egypt's prosperity and independence, and her legacy endures as a symbol of female leadership and political savvy.

In the realm of science and mathematics, Hypatia of Alexandria stands out as a pioneering figure. Living in the 4th century CE, Hypatia was a philosopher, mathematician, and astronomer who led the Neoplatonic school in Alexandria. Her work in mathematics and her teachings on philosophy made her one of the most respected scholars of her time. Hypatia's tragic death at the hands of a mob underscores the challenges faced by women in intellectual pursuits, yet her legacy continues to inspire those who seek knowledge and truth.

The medieval period saw the rise of Joan of Arc, a peasant girl who became a national heroine of France. Claiming to have received visions from saints instructing her to support Charles VII and recover France from English domination, Joan led French forces to several important victories during the Hundred Years' War. Her unwavering faith and leadership in the face of adversity made her a symbol of courage and conviction. Despite her eventual capture and execution, Joan of Arc's legacy as a martyr and saint endures, inspiring countless individuals to stand up for their beliefs.

In the world of literature, Mary Wollstonecraft emerged as a trailblazer for women's rights. Her seminal work, "A Vindication of the Rights of

Woman," published in 1792, argued for the education and empowerment of women, challenging the prevailing notion of female inferiority. Wollstonecraft's writings laid the groundwork for feminist thought and advocacy, influencing generations of women to fight for equality and justice.

The 19th century witnessed the remarkable achievements of Harriet Tubman, an abolitionist and political activist who escaped slavery and subsequently led hundreds of enslaved people to freedom via the Underground Railroad. Tubman's courage and determination in the face of immense danger made her a key figure in the abolitionist movement. Her efforts extended beyond the Underground Railroad, as she also served as a scout and spy for the Union Army during the Civil War. Tubman's legacy as a champion of freedom and equality continues to inspire those who fight against oppression.

In the realm of politics, the 20th century saw the rise of influential women leaders such as Indira Gandhi, the first and only female Prime Minister of India. Serving from 1966 to 1977 and again from 1980 until her assassination in 1984, Gandhi was a central figure in Indian politics. Her tenure was marked by significant economic and social reforms, as well as controversial decisions such as the declaration of a state of emergency. Despite the complexities of her leadership, Gandhi's impact on Indian politics and her role as a female leader in a male-dominated arena remain significant.

The fight for civil rights in the United States was profoundly shaped by the contributions of Rosa Parks, whose refusal to give up her seat on a segregated bus in Montgomery, Alabama, sparked the Montgomery Bus Boycott. Parks' act of defiance became a catalyst for the civil rights movement, highlighting the power of individual action in the struggle for justice. Her legacy as the "mother of the civil rights movement" underscores the importance of courage and resilience in the face of systemic oppression.

In the field of science, Marie Curie's groundbreaking research on radioactivity earned her two Nobel Prizes, making her the first woman to receive the prestigious award and the only person to win Nobel Prizes in two different scientific fields. Curie's dedication to scientific discovery and her contributions to the understanding of radioactivity have had a lasting impact on the fields of physics and chemistry. Her legacy as a pioneering scientist continues to inspire women in STEM fields to pursue their passions and break barriers.

The late 20th and early 21st centuries have seen the rise of influential women in various fields, from politics to entertainment. Figures such as Malala Yousafzai, the youngest Nobel Prize laureate, have become symbols of the fight for girls' education and empowerment. Malala's advocacy for education in the face of adversity has inspired a global movement for gender equality and access to education for all children.

In the arts, figures like Frida Kahlo have left an indelible mark on the world of visual art. Kahlo's unique style and exploration of identity, postcolonialism, and gender have made her an icon of artistic expression and feminist thought. Her work continues to resonate with audiences worldwide, challenging traditional notions of beauty and identity.

Patriarchy and Its Impact

Patriarchy, a social system in which men hold primary power and predominate in roles of political leadership, moral authority, and control over property, has been a defining feature of many societies throughout history. Its impact is far-reaching, influencing not only the structures of power and authority but also the everyday lives of individuals. Understanding the implications of patriarchy is essential for addressing the inequalities it perpetuates and for fostering a more equitable society.

The roots of patriarchy can be traced back to ancient civilizations, where male dominance was often institutionalized through laws, customs, and religious doctrines. These systems were designed to maintain male authority and control, often at the expense of women's rights and autonomy. In many cultures, women were relegated to the domestic sphere, their roles defined by their relationships to men as daughters, wives, and mothers. This division of labor and power was reinforced by cultural narratives that emphasized male superiority and female subservience.

One of the most significant impacts of patriarchy is the perpetuation of gender inequality. Patriarchal systems often prioritize male interests and perspectives, leading to disparities in access to resources, opportunities, and decision-making power.

This inequality is evident in various aspects of society, from the gender pay gap and underrepresentation of women in leadership positions to the prevalence of gender-based violence and discrimination. These disparities not only limit the potential of individuals but also hinder social and economic progress.

Patriarchy also shapes societal norms and expectations, influencing how individuals perceive themselves and others. Traditional gender roles, which dictate how men and women should behave, are often rooted in patriarchal values. Men are typically expected to be assertive, competitive, and dominant, while women are encouraged to be nurturing, passive, and submissive. These stereotypes can limit personal expression and development, as individuals may feel pressured to conform to societal expectations rather than pursue their true interests and talents.

The impact of patriarchy extends to the realm of politics and governance, where male dominance is often reflected in the composition of political institutions and decision-making bodies. Women's underrepresentation in politics is a significant barrier to achieving gender equality, as it limits the diversity of perspectives and experiences that inform policy-making processes. This lack of representation can result in policies that fail to address the specific needs and challenges faced by women and gender minorities, perpetuating existing inequalities.

In the economic sphere, patriarchy influences the distribution of wealth and resources, often to the detriment of women and marginalized communities. The gender pay gap, which persists across industries and regions, is a stark example of how patriarchal systems devalue women's work and contributions. Women are often concentrated in lower-paying jobs and sectors, with limited opportunities for advancement and leadership. This economic inequality is further compounded by the disproportionate burden of unpaid care work, which is often shouldered by women and undervalued by society.

Patriarchy also has profound implications for personal relationships and family structures. Power imbalances in romantic relationships, marriages, and families can create dynamics that are harmful and oppressive. Traditional notions of male authority and female submission can lead to patterns of control and abuse, undermining the autonomy and well-being of individuals. Challenging these dynamics requires a commitment to promoting equality and respect within relationships, as well as supporting individuals in their pursuit of autonomy and agency.

Despite the pervasive influence of patriarchy, there have been significant efforts to challenge and dismantle its structures. Feminist movements, which have emerged in various forms throughout history, have been instrumental in advocating for gender equality and challenging patriarchal norms. These movements have achieved significant victories, from securing women's suffrage and reproductive rights to advancing gender equality in education and the workplace. However, the struggle for equality is ongoing, as patriarchal systems continue to adapt and persist in new forms.

Addressing the impact of patriarchy requires a multifaceted approach that involves individuals, communities, and institutions. Education plays a crucial role in challenging patriarchal norms and promoting gender equality. By fostering critical thinking and encouraging individuals to question traditional gender roles, education can empower individuals to challenge oppressive systems and advocate for change. This includes promoting diverse perspectives and experiences, as well as providing opportunities for marginalized communities to have their voices heard and valued.

Policy and governance are also critical areas for addressing the impact of patriarchy. Gender-responsive policies that address the specific needs and challenges faced by women and gender minorities are essential for promoting equality and empowerment. This includes policies related to reproductive rights, workplace equality, and protection against gender-based violence. By incorporating gender perspectives into policy-making processes, governments and organizations can create more equitable and just societies.

In the realm of personal relationships, challenging patriarchal dynamics involves promoting open and honest communication, mutual respect, and equality. This includes challenging traditional gender roles and expectations, supporting each other's autonomy and agency, and fostering environments where individuals can express themselves freely and authentically. By building relationships that are based on equality and respect, individuals can create spaces where power is shared and exercised in ways that reflect the diversity and complexity of human experiences.

Feminist Movements and Power Shifts

The history of feminist movements is a testament to the power of collective action and the relentless pursuit of equality and justice. These movements have been instrumental in challenging entrenched power structures and advocating for the rights and empowerment of women and gender minorities. By examining the evolution of feminist movements and the power shifts they have engendered, we gain insight into the ongoing struggle for gender equality and the transformative potential of activism.

The roots of feminist movements can be traced back to the late 18th and early 19th centuries, a period marked by significant social and political upheaval. The Enlightenment's emphasis on reason and individual rights laid the groundwork for early feminist thought, as women began to question their exclusion from the rights and privileges afforded to men. Figures such as Mary Wollstonecraft emerged as pioneers of feminist advocacy, challenging the prevailing notion of female inferiority and arguing for women's education and empowerment. Her seminal work, "A Vindication of the Rights of Woman," published in 1792, laid the foundation for future feminist movements by articulating the need for gender equality and the dismantling of patriarchal structures.

The 19th century saw the rise of the first wave of feminism, which focused primarily on legal issues such as women's suffrage and property rights. This period was characterized by organized efforts to secure the right to vote for women, a struggle that spanned decades and involved countless activists and organizations. In the United States, figures like Susan B. Anthony and Elizabeth Cady Stanton played pivotal roles in the suffrage movement, organizing conventions, delivering speeches, and lobbying for legislative change. Their efforts culminated in the passage of the 19th Amendment in 1920, granting women the right to vote and marking a significant victory for the feminist movement.

Across the Atlantic, the suffrage movement in the United Kingdom was equally fervent, with activists such as Emmeline Pankhurst and the Women's Social and Political Union employing militant tactics to draw attention to their cause. The suffragettes' determination and resilience in the face of opposition and imprisonment underscored the urgency of their demands and ultimately contributed to the passage of the Representation of the People Act in 1918, which extended voting rights to women over the age of 30.

The achievements of the first wave of feminism laid the groundwork for subsequent movements, as women continued to challenge the social, economic, and political inequalities that persisted despite legal victories. The mid-20th century witnessed the emergence of the second wave of feminism, which expanded the focus beyond legal rights to address broader issues of gender inequality, including workplace discrimination, reproductive rights, and sexual liberation. This period was marked by a growing awareness of the systemic nature of gender oppression and the need for comprehensive social change.

The second wave of feminism was characterized by a diverse array of voices and perspectives, reflecting the complexity of women's experiences and the intersections of race, class, and sexuality. In the United States, the publication of Betty Friedan's "The Feminine Mystique" in 1963 is often credited with sparking the second wave, as it articulated the dissatisfaction and discontent felt by many women confined to traditional domestic roles. Friedan's work, along with the activism of organizations such as the National Organization for Women (NOW), helped to galvanize a movement that sought to challenge the status quo and advocate for gender equality in all aspects of life.

The second wave also saw the rise of radical feminism, which sought to address the root causes of gender oppression and challenge the patriarchal structures that underpinned society. Radical feminists argued for a fundamental reordering of social and political systems, advocating for women's autonomy and the dismantling of traditional gender roles. This period was marked by significant activism and advocacy, as women organized protests, consciousness-raising groups, and campaigns to address issues such as reproductive rights, sexual violence, and workplace discrimination.

The achievements of the second wave of feminism were significant, resulting in landmark legislation such as the Equal Pay Act, Title IX, and the Roe v.

Wade decision, which recognized women's right to reproductive autonomy. These victories represented important shifts in power, as women gained greater control over their bodies, careers, and lives. However, the movement also faced criticism for its lack of inclusivity and its failure to adequately address the experiences of women of color, working-class women, and LGBTQ+ individuals.

The late 20th century saw the emergence of the third wave of feminism, which sought to address these shortcomings and embrace a more inclusive and intersectional approach to gender equality. Third-wave feminists emphasized the diversity of women's experiences and the need to consider the intersections of race, class, sexuality, and gender identity in the fight for equality. This period was characterized by a focus on individual empowerment and the celebration of diverse expressions of femininity and identity.

The third wave of feminism also embraced the use of digital platforms and social media as tools for activism and advocacy, creating new opportunities for individuals to connect, organize, and amplify their voices. This shift in tactics reflected the changing landscape of activism and the potential for technology to facilitate social change. The rise of online communities and movements, such as the #MeToo movement, highlighted the power of collective action and the importance of creating spaces for marginalized voices to be heard and valued.

As we move into the 21st century, feminist movements continue to evolve and adapt to the changing social and political landscape. The fourth wave of feminism, characterized by its focus on intersectionality, inclusivity, and global solidarity, seeks to address the ongoing challenges of gender inequality and advocate for systemic change. This wave emphasizes the importance of addressing issues such as gender-based violence, reproductive rights, and economic inequality, while also recognizing the interconnectedness of struggles for justice and equality across different communities and contexts.

Lessons from Historical Gender Dynamics

The tapestry of human history is woven with the intricate threads of gender dynamics, each era offering unique lessons that continue to resonate in contemporary society. By examining historical gender dynamics, we can glean insights into the evolution of societal norms, the resilience of individuals who challenged these norms, and the ongoing journey toward equality and justice. These lessons not only illuminate the past but also guide us in navigating the complexities of gender relations today.

In ancient societies, gender roles were often dictated by the practical needs of survival and the division of labor. In hunter-gatherer communities, men typically assumed the role of hunters, while women gathered and cared for children. This division was not rigid but rather a reflection of the community's needs and resources. The lesson here is the adaptability of gender roles, which were shaped by necessity rather than inherent superiority or inferiority. This adaptability suggests that gender roles are not fixed but can evolve in response to changing circumstances.

As societies transitioned to agriculture, the establishment of permanent settlements and the accumulation of resources led to more defined gender roles. Men often took on roles related to plowing and managing livestock, while women were responsible for domestic duties. This division was reinforced by the growing importance of property ownership and inheritance, which favored male lineage. The lesson from this period is the impact of economic structures on gender roles, highlighting how shifts in economic systems can influence societal norms and expectations.

The rise of ancient civilizations brought about the institutionalization of patriarchal systems, where men held positions of power and authority. Women were often relegated to the domestic sphere, their roles defined by their relationships to men. However, there were notable exceptions, such as in ancient Egypt, where women could own property and rule as pharaohs. This diversity underscores the lesson that gender roles are not universally fixed and can vary significantly across cultures and contexts. It also highlights the potential for women to exercise power and influence, even within patriarchal systems.

The medieval period saw the entrenchment of gender roles within the framework of feudalism and religious institutions. The Christian Church played a significant role in shaping societal norms, emphasizing virtues such as chastity and obedience for women. Despite these constraints, women found ways to exercise influence, whether through religious vocations or the management of estates. The lesson here is the resilience and agency of women, who navigated and challenged the limitations imposed by patriarchal systems. Their stories remind us of the importance of agency and the potential for individuals to effect change within restrictive environments.

The Renaissance and Enlightenment periods marked a shift in gender dynamics, as the rise of humanism emphasized education and intellectual pursuits. Women began to gain access to education and the arts, challenging traditional notions of gender roles. However, these opportunities were often limited to women of certain social classes, and the belief in male superiority persisted. The lesson from this era is the transformative power of education and the importance of challenging societal norms to create opportunities for all individuals. It also highlights the need for inclusivity and the recognition of diverse experiences in the pursuit of equality.

The industrial revolution brought about significant changes in gender dynamics, as economic and social shifts disrupted traditional family structures. The demand for labor in factories drew men away from rural areas, while women began to enter the workforce in greater numbers. This period saw the emergence of the "separate spheres" ideology, which posited distinct domains for men and women. The lesson here is the impact of economic change on gender roles and the potential for societal shifts to challenge and redefine traditional norms. It also underscores the importance of recognizing and valuing the contributions of women in all spheres of life.

The 19th and 20th centuries witnessed significant challenges to traditional gender roles, driven by social and political movements advocating for women's rights. The suffrage movement, which sought to secure the right to vote for women, was a pivotal force in challenging gender inequality. The lesson from this period is the power of collective action and advocacy in effecting change. It also highlights the importance of legal and political rights in advancing gender equality and the need for continued efforts to address systemic inequalities.

The feminist movements of the 20th century further challenged traditional gender dynamics, advocating for equality in education, employment, and reproductive rights. These movements emphasized the need to address the systemic nature of gender oppression and the importance of intersectionality in understanding diverse experiences. The lesson here is the importance of recognizing and addressing the interconnectedness of various forms of oppression and the need for inclusive and intersectional approaches to advocacy and activism.

In contemporary society, gender dynamics continue to evolve, influenced by ongoing social movements, technological advancements, and cultural shifts. The rise of digital platforms and social media has transformed the ways in which gender is expressed and perceived, creating new opportunities for individuals to challenge traditional norms and advocate for change. The lesson from this period is the potential for technology to facilitate social change and the importance of creating spaces for diverse voices and experiences to be heard and valued.

Despite these advances, challenges remain. Gender dynamics continue to be a site of contestation and negotiation, as individuals and communities grapple with the legacy of historical inequalities and the need for continued progress. The lesson here is the importance of ongoing efforts to promote equality and empowerment for all individuals. By understanding the evolution of gender dynamics through history, we can better appreciate the complexities of gender relations and the importance of continued advocacy and activism in the pursuit of a more just and equitable world.

Chapter 3

Theories of Gender and Power

Sociological Theories on Gender

Sociological theories on gender offer a rich tapestry of perspectives that help us understand the complex ways in which gender shapes and is shaped by society. These theories provide frameworks for analyzing the social construction of gender, the power dynamics at play, and the implications for individuals and communities. By examining these theories, we gain insight into the multifaceted nature of gender and the ongoing quest for equality and justice.

One of the foundational theories in the sociology of gender is the social constructionist perspective. This theory posits that gender is not an innate biological characteristic but rather a social construct that is created and maintained through social interactions and cultural norms. According to this view, gender roles and expectations are learned behaviors that are reinforced through socialization processes, such as family upbringing, education, and media representation. The social constructionist perspective challenges the notion of fixed gender identities and highlights the fluidity and variability of gender across different cultures and historical periods.

The concept of "doing gender," introduced by sociologists Candace West and Don Zimmerman, further elaborates on the social constructionist perspective. This theory suggests that gender is an ongoing performance, enacted through everyday interactions and behaviors. Individuals "do gender" by conforming to societal expectations and norms, thereby reinforcing the existing gender order. This perspective emphasizes the active role individuals play in constructing and perpetuating gender norms, as well as the potential for resistance and change.

Structural functionalism, another sociological theory, offers a different lens through which to view gender. This perspective views society as a complex system composed of interrelated parts, each serving a specific function to maintain social stability and order. From a functionalist standpoint, traditional gender roles are seen as necessary for the smooth functioning of society, with men and women occupying complementary roles that contribute to the overall stability of the family and community. While this perspective has been criticized for reinforcing gender stereotypes and justifying inequality, it provides insight into the ways in which gender roles have been institutionalized and maintained over time.

Conflict theory, rooted in the work of Karl Marx, offers a critical perspective on gender by focusing on the power dynamics and inequalities inherent in social structures. This theory posits that gender inequality is a result of the unequal distribution of power and resources, with men historically occupying positions of dominance and control. Conflict theorists argue that gender roles and norms serve to perpetuate this inequality, benefiting those in power while marginalizing and oppressing others. This perspective highlights the importance of examining the intersections of gender with other forms of inequality, such as class and race, to understand the complexities of power and oppression.

Feminist theory, which encompasses a diverse range of perspectives, is central to the sociological study of gender. Feminist theorists challenge traditional notions of gender and advocate for the dismantling of patriarchal systems that perpetuate inequality and oppression. Key strands of feminist theory include liberal feminism, which focuses on achieving gender equality through legal and political reforms; radical feminism, which seeks to address the root causes of gender oppression and advocate for a fundamental reordering of society; and intersectional feminism, which emphasizes the interconnectedness of various forms of oppression and the need for inclusive and diverse approaches to advocacy and activism.

Intersectionality, a concept introduced by Kimberlé Crenshaw, has become a critical framework within feminist theory and the sociology of gender. This perspective emphasizes the importance of considering the intersections of gender with other social identities, such as race, class, sexuality, and ability, to understand the complexity of individual experiences and the multifaceted nature of oppression. Intersectionality challenges the notion of a singular, universal experience of gender and highlights the need for nuanced and inclusive approaches to social justice.

Symbolic interactionism, another sociological theory, focuses on the micro-level interactions and meanings that shape individual identities and social realities. From this perspective, gender is understood as a set of symbols and meanings that are negotiated and constructed through social interactions. Symbolic interactionists emphasize the importance of language, symbols, and communication in shaping gender identities and roles. This perspective highlights the fluidity and variability of gender, as individuals actively construct and negotiate their identities in response to social cues and expectations.

Queer theory, which emerged in the late 20th century, challenges traditional binary notions of gender and sexuality. This perspective critiques the rigid categorization of individuals into fixed gender and sexual identities and emphasizes the fluidity and diversity of human experiences. Queer theorists argue for the deconstruction of normative gender and sexual categories, advocating for a more inclusive and expansive understanding of identity. This perspective highlights the potential for resistance and transformation, as individuals challenge and subvert traditional norms and expectations.

The sociological theories on gender provide valuable insights into the complex and dynamic nature of gender in society. They offer frameworks for understanding the social construction of gender, the power dynamics at play, and the implications for individuals and communities. By examining these theories, we gain a deeper understanding of the multifaceted nature of gender and the ongoing quest for equality and justice. These perspectives remind us of the importance of challenging traditional norms and advocating for inclusive and diverse approaches to social change.

In contemporary society, the application of these sociological theories is essential for addressing the ongoing challenges of gender inequality and advocating for systemic change. By recognizing the social construction of gender and the power dynamics at play, we can work towards creating more equitable and just societies. This requires a commitment to challenging traditional norms, advocating for inclusive and intersectional approaches to social justice, and creating spaces for diverse voices and experiences to be heard and valued.

Psychological Perspectives on Power

Power, an omnipresent force in human interactions, is a concept that has intrigued psychologists for decades. It influences relationships, shapes identities, and dictates social dynamics. Understanding the psychological perspectives on power provides valuable insights into how individuals perceive, wield, and respond to power in various contexts. This exploration delves into the intricacies of power from a psychological standpoint, offering practical insights for navigating its complexities.

At its core, power is the ability to influence or control the behavior of others. Psychologists have long been interested in the origins and manifestations of power, examining how it affects individuals' thoughts, emotions, and behaviors. One of the foundational theories in this domain is the social power theory, which categorizes power into different bases: coercive, reward, legitimate, referent, and expert power. Each base represents a distinct source of influence, from the ability to administer punishments or rewards to the possession of specialized knowledge or skills.

Coercive power, derived from the capacity to impose penalties or sanctions, often evokes fear and compliance. It is a form of power that can lead to resentment and resistance if overused or perceived as unjust. Reward power, on the other hand, stems from the ability to provide incentives or benefits. While it can foster motivation and cooperation, it may also create dependency and diminish intrinsic motivation if not balanced with other forms of influence.

Legitimate power is rooted in formal authority or position, often recognized and accepted by others. It is the power of leaders, managers, and officials, conferred by organizational structures or societal norms. This form of power can be effective in establishing order and facilitating decision-making, but it requires legitimacy and trust to be sustainable. Referent power, based on admiration or identification with an individual, is a more personal form of influence. It is the power of role models and charismatic leaders, who inspire others through their qualities and actions.

Expert power arises from the possession of specialized knowledge or skills, granting individuals influence in areas where their expertise is recognized and valued. This form of power is particularly relevant in professional and academic settings, where expertise is a key determinant of credibility and authority. However, it requires continuous learning and adaptation to maintain its relevance and effectiveness.

The psychological impact of power on individuals is profound, influencing their self-perception, behavior, and interactions with others. Research has shown that power can enhance confidence, assertiveness, and risk-taking, as individuals with power often feel more in control of their environment and outcomes. However, power can also lead to overconfidence, insensitivity, and ethical lapses, as individuals may become less attuned to the perspectives and needs of others.

The concept of power distance, introduced by social psychologist Geert Hofstede, further elucidates the psychological dynamics of power. Power distance refers to the extent to which individuals in a society accept and expect unequal distribution of power. In high power distance cultures, hierarchical structures are more pronounced, and authority is often unquestioned. In contrast, low power distance cultures emphasize equality and participatory decision-making, with power being more evenly distributed.

Understanding power distance is crucial for navigating cross-cultural interactions and fostering effective communication. In high power distance settings, individuals may need to adopt a more formal and respectful approach, acknowledging authority and hierarchy. In low power distance contexts, open dialogue and collaboration are often valued, with an emphasis on egalitarianism and shared decision-making.

The psychological effects of power are not limited to those who possess it; they also extend to those who are subject to it. Power dynamics can shape individuals' perceptions of fairness, autonomy, and agency, influencing their motivation, satisfaction, and well-being. When power is perceived as legitimate and fair, it can foster trust, cooperation, and commitment. Conversely, when power is seen as arbitrary or oppressive, it can lead to resistance, disengagement, and conflict.

The interplay between power and identity is another critical aspect of psychological perspectives on power. Power can shape individuals' self-concept and social identity, influencing how they see themselves and how they are perceived by others. For those in positions of power, identity may be closely tied to their role and authority, affecting their sense of self-worth and purpose. For those without power, identity may be shaped by experiences of marginalization or exclusion, impacting their self-esteem and aspirations.

Empowerment, a concept closely related to power, is a psychological process that involves gaining control, confidence, and agency. Empowerment is not merely the absence of powerlessness but the active pursuit of self-determination and influence. It involves recognizing one's strengths, capabilities, and potential, as well as challenging the barriers and constraints that limit one's power. Empowerment can occur at individual, organizational, and societal levels, fostering resilience, innovation, and social change.

The role of power in relationships is another area of interest for psychologists, as power dynamics can significantly impact interpersonal interactions and outcomes. In healthy relationships, power is often balanced and shared, with both parties having a voice and influence. However, imbalances of power can lead to conflict, manipulation, and abuse, undermining trust and intimacy. Understanding the psychological dynamics of power in relationships is essential for fostering healthy and equitable interactions.

Effective communication is a key factor in managing power dynamics and promoting positive outcomes. Active listening, empathy, and assertiveness are essential skills for navigating power relations, as they facilitate understanding, respect, and collaboration. By recognizing and addressing power imbalances, individuals can create more inclusive and empowering environments, where diverse perspectives and contributions are valued.

The psychological perspectives on power offer valuable insights into the complexities of human interactions and the potential for growth and transformation. By understanding the different bases of power, the impact of power on individuals and relationships, and the role of power distance and empowerment, we can navigate the challenges and opportunities of power with greater awareness and intention. These insights remind us of the importance of ethical and responsible use of power, as well as the potential for empowerment and positive change.

Feminist Theory and Power Dynamics

Feminist theory offers a profound lens through which to examine power dynamics, challenging traditional structures and advocating for a more equitable society. At its core, feminist theory seeks to understand and dismantle the systems of oppression that have historically marginalized women and gender minorities. By exploring the intersections of gender, power, and society, feminist theory provides a framework for analyzing the complexities of power dynamics and envisioning transformative change.

The roots of feminist theory can be traced back to the early feminist movements of the 19th and 20th centuries, which sought to address the legal and social inequalities faced by women. These movements laid the groundwork for the development of feminist thought, as activists and scholars began to articulate the need for a comprehensive understanding of gender and power. The emergence of feminist theory marked a significant shift in the discourse, as it moved beyond the pursuit of legal rights to address the broader social, cultural, and economic dimensions of gender inequality.

One of the foundational concepts in feminist theory is the notion of patriarchy, a system of power that privileges men and subordinates women. Patriarchy is not merely a collection of individual attitudes or behaviors but a pervasive social structure that shapes institutions, norms, and practices. Feminist theorists argue that patriarchy is maintained through various mechanisms, including cultural narratives, legal systems, and economic structures, which reinforce gender hierarchies and limit women's agency.

The concept of intersectionality, introduced by Kimberlé Crenshaw, has become a cornerstone of feminist theory, emphasizing the interconnectedness of various forms of oppression. Intersectionality challenges the notion of a singular, universal experience of gender and highlights the need to consider the intersections of race, class, sexuality, and other social identities in understanding power dynamics. This perspective underscores the importance of recognizing and valuing diverse experiences and perspectives in the pursuit of equality and justice.

Feminist theory also critiques the traditional binary understanding of gender, advocating for a more inclusive and expansive view of identity. Queer theory, which emerged in the late 20th century, aligns with feminist thought in challenging rigid categorizations of gender and sexuality. By deconstructing normative gender and sexual categories, queer theorists advocate for a more fluid and diverse understanding of identity, highlighting the potential for resistance and transformation.

The exploration of power dynamics within feminist theory extends to the analysis of language and representation. Language is a powerful tool that shapes perceptions and reinforces social norms. Feminist theorists argue that language can perpetuate gender stereotypes and marginalize women's voices, emphasizing the need for inclusive and equitable representation. This critique extends to media and cultural narratives, which often reflect and reinforce patriarchal values. By challenging these narratives, feminist theory seeks to create spaces for diverse voices and stories to be heard and valued.

Feminist theory also examines the role of power in relationships, both personal and institutional. In personal relationships, power dynamics can manifest in various ways, from decision-making and communication to emotional and physical control. Feminist theorists advocate for egalitarian relationships, where power is shared and both parties have a voice and influence. This perspective emphasizes the importance of mutual respect, empathy, and collaboration in fostering healthy and equitable interactions.

At the institutional level, feminist theory critiques the power structures that perpetuate gender inequality, from workplaces and educational institutions to legal and political systems. By analyzing the ways in which power is distributed and exercised, feminist theorists seek to identify and challenge the barriers that limit women's opportunities and agency. This critique extends to the economic sphere, where gender disparities in pay, employment, and leadership positions reflect broader systemic inequalities.

The concept of empowerment is central to feminist theory, emphasizing the importance of agency and self-determination. Empowerment is not merely the absence of powerlessness but the active pursuit of influence and control over one's life. Feminist theorists argue that empowerment involves recognizing one's strengths and capabilities, as well as challenging the barriers and constraints that limit one's power. This perspective highlights the potential for individuals and communities to effect change and create more equitable and just societies.

Feminist theory also emphasizes the importance of collective action and solidarity in challenging power dynamics and advocating for social change. The history of feminist movements is a testament to the power of collective action, as individuals and communities have come together to challenge oppression and advocate for equality. This perspective underscores the importance of building alliances and coalitions across diverse communities and movements, recognizing the interconnectedness of struggles for justice and equality.

In contemporary society, feminist theory continues to evolve and adapt to the changing social and political landscape. The rise of digital platforms and social media has transformed the ways in which feminist activism is conducted, creating new opportunities for individuals to connect, organize, and amplify their voices. This shift reflects the changing nature of power dynamics and the potential for technology to facilitate social change.

Despite the progress made, challenges remain. Gender inequality persists in various forms, from violence and discrimination to economic and political disparities. Feminist theory reminds us of the importance of ongoing efforts to challenge traditional norms and advocate for inclusive and diverse approaches to social justice. By recognizing the complexities of power dynamics and the potential for transformation, we can work towards creating a more equitable and just world for all individuals.

The insights from feminist theory offer valuable perspectives on the complexities of power dynamics and the potential for growth and transformation. By understanding the intersections of gender, power, and society, we can navigate the challenges and opportunities of power with greater awareness and intention. These insights remind us of the importance of ethical and responsible use of power, as well as the potential for empowerment and positive change.

Intersectionality and Power Structures

Intersectionality, a term coined by legal scholar Kimberlé Crenshaw, offers a vital framework for understanding the complex interplay of power structures that shape individual experiences and societal dynamics. At its essence, intersectionality acknowledges that individuals are not defined by a single identity, such as gender or race, but rather by a multitude of intersecting identities that collectively influence their experiences of privilege and oppression. This perspective challenges the notion of a singular, universal experience and emphasizes the need to consider the interconnectedness of various forms of social stratification.

The concept of intersectionality emerged from the recognition that traditional approaches to social justice often failed to address the unique challenges faced by individuals who occupy multiple marginalized identities. For instance, the experiences of a Black woman cannot be fully understood by examining race and gender separately, as these identities intersect to create distinct experiences of discrimination and inequality. Intersectionality thus provides a more nuanced and comprehensive understanding of power structures, highlighting the importance of considering the full spectrum of identities and experiences in the pursuit of equality and justice.

Power structures, whether they manifest in institutions, cultural norms, or interpersonal relationships, are often complex and multifaceted. They are shaped by historical, social, and economic forces that create and perpetuate hierarchies of privilege and oppression. Intersectionality offers a lens through which to examine these power structures, revealing the ways in which they intersect and interact to shape individual experiences and societal outcomes.

One of the key insights of intersectionality is the recognition that power is not monolithic but rather distributed across multiple axes of identity. This means that individuals can experience both privilege and oppression simultaneously, depending on the context and the specific identities at play. For example, a white woman may experience gender-based discrimination while simultaneously benefiting from racial privilege. This duality underscores the importance of examining power structures in their entirety, rather than focusing on a single axis of identity.

The application of intersectionality extends beyond individual experiences to encompass broader societal dynamics. By examining the intersections of race, gender, class, sexuality, ability, and other identities, intersectionality reveals the systemic nature of inequality and the ways in which power structures are reinforced and perpetuated. This perspective challenges traditional approaches to social justice that often prioritize one form of oppression over others, advocating instead for a more inclusive and holistic approach that addresses the full complexity of power dynamics.

Intersectionality also highlights the importance of recognizing and valuing diverse experiences and perspectives in the pursuit of social change. By centering the voices and experiences of those who occupy multiple marginalized identities, intersectionality challenges dominant narratives and creates space for more inclusive and equitable approaches to advocacy and activism. This perspective emphasizes the need for solidarity and coalition-building across diverse communities and movements, recognizing the interconnectedness of struggles for justice and equality.

In practice, applying an intersectional lens to power structures requires a commitment to examining and addressing the root causes of inequality. This involves challenging the systemic barriers and constraints that limit individuals' opportunities and agency, as well as recognizing the ways in which power is distributed and exercised. It also requires a willingness to engage in critical self-reflection and to confront one's own privilege and biases, acknowledging the ways in which they may contribute to the perpetuation of inequality.

Intersectionality also calls for a reimagining of traditional power structures and the creation of more inclusive and equitable systems. This involves challenging hierarchical and exclusionary practices and advocating for policies and practices that promote diversity, equity, and inclusion. By recognizing the value of diverse perspectives and experiences, intersectionality fosters innovation and creativity, creating opportunities for individuals and communities to thrive and contribute to the collective well-being of society.

The insights from intersectionality offer valuable guidance for navigating the complexities of power structures and advocating for transformative change. By understanding the interconnectedness of identities and the systemic nature of inequality, we can work towards creating more equitable and just societies. This requires a commitment to challenging traditional norms and advocating for inclusive and diverse approaches to social justice, recognizing the potential for empowerment and positive change.

In contemporary society, the application of intersectionality is essential for addressing the ongoing challenges of inequality and advocating for systemic change. The rise of digital platforms and social media has transformed the ways in which intersectional activism is conducted, creating new opportunities for individuals to connect, organize, and amplify their voices. This shift reflects the changing nature of power dynamics and the potential for technology to facilitate social change.

Despite the progress made, challenges remain. Intersectionality reminds us of the importance of ongoing efforts to challenge traditional norms and advocate for inclusive and diverse approaches to social justice. By recognizing the complexities of power dynamics and the potential for transformation, we can work towards creating a more equitable and just world for all individuals.

The insights from intersectionality offer valuable perspectives on the complexities of power structures

and the potential for growth and transformation. By
understanding the intersections of identities and the
systemic nature of inequality, we can navigate the
challenges and opportunities of power with greater
awareness and intention. These insights remind us of
the importance of ethical and responsible use of
power, as well as the potential for empowerment and
positive change.

Critiques and Debates in Gender Theory

Gender theory, a dynamic and evolving field, has
sparked numerous critiques and debates over the
years. These discussions are essential for the growth
and refinement of the discipline, as they challenge
existing paradigms and encourage the exploration of
new perspectives. By examining these critiques and
debates, we gain a deeper understanding of the
complexities of gender and the diverse ways in which
it is experienced and understood.

One of the central debates in gender theory revolves
around the concept of gender as a social construct.
While many theorists argue that gender is not an
inherent biological trait but rather a product of
socialization and cultural norms, others contend that
this perspective overlooks the role of biology in
shaping gender identity and expression. This debate
highlights the tension between nature and nurture,
raising questions about the extent to which gender is
determined by biological factors versus social
influences.

The critique of essentialism is another significant point of contention within gender theory. Essentialism posits that certain characteristics or traits are inherent to specific genders, often reinforcing traditional stereotypes and limiting the diversity of gender expressions. Critics argue that essentialist views perpetuate rigid binaries and fail to account for the fluidity and variability of gender across different cultures and historical contexts. This critique has led to the development of more inclusive and expansive understandings of gender, emphasizing the importance of recognizing and valuing diverse identities and experiences.

The rise of queer theory has further complicated traditional notions of gender, challenging the binary framework that has long dominated the discourse. Queer theorists argue that gender and sexuality are not fixed categories but rather fluid and dynamic constructs that can be deconstructed and reimagined. This perspective has sparked debates about the boundaries of gender and the potential for resistance and transformation. While some critics argue that queer theory's emphasis on deconstruction can undermine efforts to address concrete issues of inequality and discrimination, others contend that it offers valuable insights into the complexities of identity and the potential for social change.

Intersectionality, a concept that has gained prominence in recent years, has also generated significant debate within gender theory. While intersectionality emphasizes the interconnectedness of various forms of oppression and the need to consider multiple identities in understanding power dynamics, some critics argue that it can lead to a fragmentation of the feminist movement. They contend that focusing on individual identities and experiences can detract from the pursuit of collective goals and dilute the impact of advocacy efforts. However, proponents of intersectionality argue that it offers a more comprehensive and inclusive approach to social justice, recognizing the diversity of experiences and the need for solidarity across different communities and movements.

The debate over the role of language and representation in shaping gender identities and norms is another critical area of discussion within gender theory. Language is a powerful tool that can both reflect and reinforce social norms, and feminist theorists have long critiqued the ways in which language can marginalize and silence women's voices. This critique extends to media and cultural narratives, which often perpetuate gender stereotypes and limit the visibility of diverse identities. While some argue that changing language and representation is essential for challenging traditional norms and promoting inclusivity, others contend that these efforts can be superficial and fail to address the root causes of inequality.

The tension between theory and practice is another ongoing debate within gender theory. While theoretical frameworks provide valuable insights into the complexities of gender and power, critics argue that they can be disconnected from the lived experiences of individuals and the practical realities of advocacy and activism. This critique highlights the importance of bridging the gap between theory and practice, ensuring that theoretical insights are grounded in real-world experiences and inform meaningful action.

The role of gender theory in shaping policy and social change is another area of debate. While gender theory has contributed to significant advancements in legal and social rights, critics argue that its impact can be limited by institutional and cultural resistance. This critique underscores the importance of translating theoretical insights into concrete policy changes and advocating for systemic reform. It also highlights the need for ongoing efforts to challenge traditional norms and structures, recognizing the potential for transformation and the importance of sustained advocacy and activism.

The critiques and debates within gender theory offer valuable insights into the complexities of gender and the diverse ways in which it is experienced and understood. By engaging with these discussions, we can refine and expand our understanding of gender, recognizing the importance of diverse perspectives and experiences in shaping the discourse. These debates remind us of the importance of ongoing efforts to challenge traditional norms and advocate for inclusive and diverse approaches to social justice.

In contemporary society, the application of gender theory is essential for addressing the ongoing challenges of inequality and advocating for systemic change. By recognizing the complexities of gender and the potential for transformation, we can work towards creating more equitable and just societies. This requires a commitment to challenging traditional norms and advocating for inclusive and diverse approaches to social justice, recognizing the potential for empowerment and positive change.

The insights from critiques and debates in gender theory offer valuable perspectives on the complexities of gender and the potential for growth and transformation. By understanding the diverse ways in which gender is experienced and understood, we can navigate the challenges and opportunities of power with greater awareness and intention. These insights remind us of the importance of ethical and responsible use of power, as well as the potential for empowerment and positive change.

Chapter 4

Gender and Power in the Workplace

Gender Disparities in Leadership

Harnessing the power of the wind has long been a pursuit of human ingenuity, and with the growing emphasis on sustainable energy, small-scale wind systems for home use have gained significant attention. These systems offer a promising solution for homeowners seeking to reduce their carbon footprint and achieve energy independence. Understanding the intricacies of small-scale wind systems, from their components to their installation and maintenance, is essential for anyone considering this renewable energy option.

At the heart of any wind energy system is the wind turbine, a device that converts the kinetic energy of the wind into electrical energy. Small-scale wind turbines, designed for residential use, typically have a capacity ranging from a few hundred watts to several kilowatts. These turbines can be mounted on rooftops or standalone towers, depending on the available space and wind conditions. The choice of turbine size and type is influenced by factors such as average wind speed, energy needs, and budget.

The efficiency of a wind turbine is largely determined by its location. Wind speed and consistency are critical factors in maximizing energy production. Ideally, a wind turbine should be situated in an area with unobstructed access to prevailing winds, away from buildings, trees, and other obstacles that can create turbulence and reduce efficiency. Conducting a thorough site assessment, including wind speed measurements and analysis of local wind patterns, is a crucial step in the planning process.

In addition to the turbine, a small-scale wind system comprises several key components, including a tower, a controller, an inverter, and a battery storage system. The tower elevates the turbine to capture stronger and more consistent winds, while the controller regulates the flow of electricity from the turbine to the inverter and battery. The inverter converts the direct current (DC) generated by the turbine into alternating current (AC), which can be used to power household appliances. A battery storage system allows homeowners to store excess energy for use during periods of low wind or high demand.

The installation of a small-scale wind system requires careful planning and consideration of various factors, including zoning regulations, permitting requirements, and potential environmental impacts. Local zoning laws may dictate the allowable height and placement of wind turbines, and obtaining the necessary permits can be a complex process. Additionally, it's important to consider the potential impact on local wildlife, particularly birds and bats, and to implement measures to mitigate any negative effects.

Once installed, a small-scale wind system requires regular maintenance to ensure optimal performance and longevity. Routine inspections of the turbine, tower, and electrical components are essential to identify and address any issues before they become significant problems. This includes checking for wear and tear on moving parts, ensuring that electrical connections are secure, and monitoring the performance of the battery storage system. Regular maintenance not only extends the lifespan of the system but also maximizes energy production and efficiency.

The financial considerations of small-scale wind systems are an important aspect for homeowners to evaluate. While the initial investment can be substantial, the long-term savings on energy bills and potential incentives, such as tax credits and rebates, can offset the costs. Additionally, the value of energy independence and the environmental benefits of reducing reliance on fossil fuels are significant factors to consider. Conducting a cost-benefit analysis, taking into account the expected energy production, installation costs, and available incentives, can help homeowners make informed decisions.

For those interested in small-scale wind systems, engaging with experienced professionals and industry experts can provide valuable insights and guidance. From site assessment and system design to installation and maintenance, working with knowledgeable professionals ensures that the system is tailored to meet the specific needs and conditions of the home. Additionally, connecting with other homeowners who have installed wind systems can offer practical advice and firsthand experiences.

The potential of small-scale wind systems extends beyond individual homes, contributing to broader efforts to promote renewable energy and sustainability. By generating clean, renewable energy, these systems help reduce greenhouse gas emissions and decrease reliance on non-renewable energy sources. As more homeowners adopt wind energy, the collective impact on the environment and energy landscape can be substantial.

In the context of a rapidly changing energy landscape, small-scale wind systems represent a viable and sustainable option for homeowners seeking to embrace renewable energy. By understanding the components, installation process, and maintenance requirements, individuals can make informed decisions and take meaningful steps towards energy independence. The journey to harnessing wind energy is not without its challenges, but the rewards of contributing to a more sustainable future are well worth the effort.

The insights gained from exploring small-scale wind systems for home use offer valuable perspectives on the potential for growth and transformation in the renewable energy sector. By recognizing the opportunities and challenges associated with wind energy, homeowners can navigate the complexities of this technology with greater awareness and intention. These insights remind us of the importance of ethical and responsible use of energy resources, as well as the potential for empowerment and positive change.

The Gender Pay Gap

The gender pay gap, a persistent issue in the global workforce, reflects the disparity in earnings between men and women. Despite decades of progress towards gender equality, this gap remains a significant barrier to economic equity and empowerment for women. Understanding the factors contributing to the gender pay gap and exploring strategies to address it are crucial steps in promoting fair and equitable compensation for all workers.

At its core, the gender pay gap is influenced by a complex interplay of factors, including occupational segregation, differences in work experience and education, and discriminatory practices. Occupational segregation refers to the concentration of men and women in different industries and job roles, often resulting in women being overrepresented in lower-paying sectors such as healthcare, education, and social services. This segregation is influenced by societal norms and expectations, which can limit women's access to higher-paying fields such as technology, engineering, and finance.

Differences in work experience and education also contribute to the gender pay gap. Women are more likely to take career breaks or work part-time due to caregiving responsibilities, which can impact their career progression and earning potential. Additionally, while women have made significant strides in educational attainment, they may still face barriers in accessing certain fields of study or advancing to leadership positions. These disparities in experience and education can result in lower earnings for women compared to their male counterparts.

Discriminatory practices, both overt and subtle, play a significant role in perpetuating the gender pay gap. These practices can include biased hiring and promotion decisions, unequal pay for equal work, and a lack of transparency in compensation practices. Unconscious biases, which operate below the level of conscious awareness, can also influence decision-making processes and contribute to pay disparities. Addressing these biases requires a commitment to raising awareness and implementing strategies to mitigate their impact, such as bias training and transparent pay practices.

The gender pay gap is not uniform across all demographics, with women of color, LGBTQ+ individuals, and women with disabilities often facing even larger disparities. Intersectionality, the interconnectedness of various forms of oppression, highlights the need to consider multiple identities in understanding and addressing the gender pay gap. Recognizing and addressing these intersecting identities is crucial for creating inclusive and equitable compensation practices that value diversity and promote equity.

Efforts to address the gender pay gap must be multifaceted and involve a combination of policy changes, organizational practices, and cultural shifts. Policy changes, such as pay equity legislation and family-friendly workplace policies, can create a framework for promoting fair compensation and supporting work-life balance. These policies can include measures such as paid parental leave, affordable childcare, and flexible work arrangements, which can help alleviate the burden of caregiving responsibilities and support women's career advancement.

Organizations play a pivotal role in addressing the gender pay gap by implementing practices that promote diversity and inclusion. This includes conducting regular pay audits to identify and address disparities, establishing transparent pay practices, and creating pathways for career advancement for women. Mentorship and sponsorship programs can also provide women with the support and guidance needed to navigate their careers and access leadership opportunities.

Cultural shifts are essential for challenging traditional norms and stereotypes that contribute to the gender pay gap. This involves promoting diverse role models and challenging societal expectations around gender roles and career choices. By fostering an inclusive culture that values diversity and promotes equity, organizations can create environments where all individuals have the opportunity to thrive and contribute to the collective success of the workforce.

The role of allies and advocates is also crucial in addressing the gender pay gap. Allies, who may be individuals in positions of power or influence, can use their privilege to support and amplify the voices of women in the workforce. This includes advocating for equitable policies, challenging biases and stereotypes, and creating opportunities for women to succeed and advance in their careers.

The insights gained from addressing the gender pay gap offer valuable perspectives on the complexities of power and the potential for growth and transformation in the workforce. By understanding the factors contributing to the pay gap and implementing strategies to address them, we can work towards creating more equitable and inclusive compensation practices. These efforts remind us of the importance of ethical and responsible use of power, as well as the potential for empowerment and positive change.

Workplace Harassment and Power Imbalance

Workplace harassment, a pervasive issue across industries, is often rooted in power imbalances that create environments ripe for abuse and discrimination. Understanding the dynamics of power in the workplace and the various forms of harassment that can arise is crucial for fostering a safe and equitable work environment. By addressing these issues head-on, organizations can create cultures of respect and accountability, where all employees feel valued and protected.

Power imbalances in the workplace can manifest in numerous ways, often stemming from hierarchical structures that place certain individuals in positions of authority over others. These imbalances can be exacerbated by factors such as gender, race, age, and socioeconomic status, creating a complex web of dynamics that can influence interactions and behaviors. When power is concentrated in the hands of a few, it can lead to an environment where harassment and discrimination are more likely to occur, as those in positions of authority may feel emboldened to exploit their power.

Harassment in the workplace can take many forms, ranging from overt acts of aggression and intimidation to more subtle behaviors that undermine an individual's dignity and sense of belonging. Sexual harassment, one of the most widely recognized forms, includes unwanted advances, inappropriate comments, and other behaviors of a sexual nature that create a hostile work environment. However, harassment can also be based on other factors, such as race, religion, disability, or sexual orientation, and can include actions such as bullying, exclusion, and microaggressions.

The impact of workplace harassment on individuals and organizations is profound. For those who experience harassment, the effects can be both psychological and physical, leading to stress, anxiety, depression, and a range of other health issues. The fear and trauma associated with harassment can also impact an individual's job performance, career progression, and overall well-being. For organizations, the consequences of harassment can include decreased productivity, increased turnover, and reputational damage, as well as potential legal and financial liabilities.

Addressing workplace harassment requires a comprehensive approach that involves policy development, education, and cultural change. Organizations must establish clear and robust anti-harassment policies that define unacceptable behaviors and outline procedures for reporting and addressing complaints. These policies should be communicated to all employees and reinforced through regular training and awareness programs that emphasize the importance of respect and inclusion.

Education and training are critical components of any anti-harassment strategy, as they help to raise awareness of the issue and equip employees with the knowledge and skills needed to recognize and respond to harassment. Training programs should be tailored to the specific needs and context of the organization and should include information on the various forms of harassment, the impact on individuals and organizations, and the steps employees can take to prevent and address harassment.

Creating a culture of respect and accountability is essential for preventing workplace harassment and addressing power imbalances. This involves fostering an environment where all employees feel empowered to speak up and report harassment without fear of retaliation. Organizations can achieve this by establishing clear reporting mechanisms, providing support and resources for those who experience harassment, and holding individuals accountable for their actions.

Leadership plays a crucial role in shaping organizational culture and setting the tone for acceptable behavior. Leaders must model respectful and inclusive behaviors and demonstrate a commitment to addressing harassment and power imbalances. This includes taking swift and appropriate action in response to complaints, as well as actively promoting diversity and inclusion initiatives that challenge traditional power structures and create opportunities for underrepresented groups.

The role of bystanders in addressing workplace harassment is also significant. Bystanders, who may witness or become aware of harassment, have the potential to intervene and support those who experience harassment. Encouraging bystander intervention through training and awareness programs can help to create a culture of collective responsibility, where all employees are empowered to take action and support their colleagues.

The insights gained from addressing workplace harassment and power imbalances offer valuable perspectives on the complexities of organizational dynamics and the potential for growth and transformation. By understanding the factors contributing to harassment and implementing strategies to address them, organizations can work towards creating more equitable and inclusive work environments. These efforts remind us of the importance of ethical and responsible use of power, as well as the potential for empowerment and positive change.

Strategies for Empowerment and Equality

Evaluating the wind potential in your area is a crucial step for anyone considering the installation of a small-scale wind energy system. Understanding the wind characteristics of your location can help determine the feasibility and potential efficiency of harnessing wind power. This process involves assessing various factors, including wind speed, direction, and consistency, as well as geographical and environmental considerations. By conducting a thorough evaluation, you can make informed decisions about the suitability of wind energy for your home or property.

The first step in evaluating wind potential is to gather data on wind speed and direction. Wind speed is a critical factor in determining the amount of energy that can be generated by a wind turbine. Generally, higher wind speeds result in greater energy production. To accurately assess wind speed, it's essential to collect data over an extended period, ideally a year or more, to account for seasonal variations and fluctuations. This data can be obtained from local weather stations, online databases, or by installing an anemometer on your property to measure wind speed directly.

In addition to wind speed, understanding wind direction is important for optimizing the placement and orientation of a wind turbine. Prevailing wind direction refers to the most common direction from which the wind blows in a particular area. By identifying the prevailing wind direction, you can position the turbine to capture the maximum amount of wind energy. Wind roses, which are graphical representations of wind direction and speed, can be useful tools for visualizing wind patterns and making informed decisions about turbine placement.

The consistency of wind is another important factor to consider when evaluating wind potential. Consistent winds provide a more reliable source of energy, while areas with highly variable or intermittent winds may not be suitable for wind energy generation. Analyzing wind consistency involves examining the frequency and duration of wind events, as well as identifying any patterns or trends that may impact energy production. This information can help determine the expected capacity factor of a wind turbine, which is a measure of its actual energy output compared to its maximum potential output.

Geographical and environmental factors also play a significant role in assessing wind potential. The topography of the land, including hills, valleys, and bodies of water, can influence wind patterns and speed. For example, wind tends to accelerate over ridges and hilltops, making these locations ideal for wind turbines. Conversely, areas with significant obstructions, such as dense forests or tall buildings, may experience reduced wind speeds and increased turbulence, which can negatively impact turbine performance.

The presence of microclimates, which are localized climate conditions that differ from the surrounding area, can also affect wind potential. Microclimates can be influenced by factors such as elevation, vegetation, and proximity to water bodies. Understanding the specific microclimate of your location can provide valuable insights into wind behavior and help identify the most suitable sites for wind energy generation.

Once you have gathered and analyzed wind data, it's important to consider the technical and economic aspects of installing a wind energy system. This includes evaluating the available space for a wind turbine, the potential energy output, and the costs associated with installation and maintenance. Conducting a cost-benefit analysis can help determine the financial viability of a wind energy project and identify any potential challenges or limitations.

In addition to technical and economic considerations, it's essential to be aware of any regulatory and permitting requirements that may apply to wind energy installations in your area. Local zoning laws, building codes, and environmental regulations can impact the feasibility of a wind energy project and may require specific approvals or permits. Engaging with local authorities and stakeholders early in the planning process can help ensure compliance and address any potential concerns.

Community engagement is another important aspect of evaluating wind potential. Wind energy projects can have social and environmental impacts, and it's important to consider the perspectives and interests of local residents and stakeholders. Engaging with the community through public meetings, consultations, and information sessions can help build support for a wind energy project and address any concerns or objections.

The insights gained from evaluating wind potential in your area offer valuable perspectives on the complexities of renewable energy and the potential for growth and transformation. By understanding the factors that influence wind behavior and implementing strategies to address them, you can make informed decisions about the suitability of wind energy for your home or property. These efforts remind us of the importance of ethical and responsible use of energy resources, as well as the potential for empowerment and positive change.

Case Studies of Gender Dynamics at Work

In the intricate tapestry of workplace dynamics, gender plays a pivotal role, influencing interactions, opportunities, and outcomes. Examining real-world case studies of gender dynamics at work provides valuable insights into the challenges and successes experienced by individuals and organizations striving for equality. These stories illuminate the complexities of gender in the workplace and offer lessons that can guide efforts to create more inclusive and equitable environments.

One notable case involves a multinational technology company that embarked on a journey to address gender disparities within its workforce. Despite being a leader in innovation, the company faced criticism for its lack of gender diversity, particularly in technical and leadership roles. In response, the company launched a comprehensive initiative aimed at increasing the representation of women across all levels. This initiative included targeted recruitment efforts, mentorship programs, and leadership development opportunities for women. Over time, the company saw a significant increase in the number of women in technical roles and leadership positions, demonstrating the impact of intentional and sustained efforts to promote gender diversity.

Another compelling case study highlights the experiences of a female executive in the finance industry, a sector traditionally dominated by men. Despite her qualifications and achievements, she encountered numerous barriers to advancement, including biased assumptions about her capabilities and a lack of access to influential networks. Determined to succeed, she leveraged her expertise and built a strong support network of mentors and allies. Her perseverance paid off, as she eventually rose to a senior leadership position, where she became a vocal advocate for gender equality and mentorship for other women in the industry. Her story underscores the importance of resilience and the power of mentorship in overcoming gender-based obstacles.

In contrast, a case study from the healthcare sector reveals the challenges faced by male nurses in a predominantly female profession. Despite the growing demand for nurses, men in the field often encounter stereotypes and biases that question their suitability for caregiving roles. One male nurse shared his experiences of being perceived as less compassionate or nurturing than his female colleagues, despite his dedication and competence. To address these challenges, he became involved in initiatives to promote diversity and inclusion within the nursing profession, advocating for the recognition of diverse skills and perspectives. His efforts contributed to a more inclusive environment where all nurses, regardless of gender, were valued for their contributions.

A case from the creative industry illustrates the impact of gender dynamics on collaboration and creativity. A mixed-gender team working on a high-profile advertising campaign experienced tension and conflict due to differing communication styles and expectations. The team leader, recognizing the potential for gender dynamics to influence team interactions, facilitated open discussions about communication preferences and encouraged team members to share their perspectives. By fostering an environment of mutual respect and understanding, the team was able to harness their diverse strengths and produce a successful campaign that resonated with a wide audience. This case highlights the importance of addressing gender dynamics in collaborative settings to enhance creativity and innovation.

In the realm of academia, a case study explores the experiences of women in STEM (science, technology, engineering, and mathematics) fields. Despite efforts to increase female representation, women in STEM often face challenges such as gender bias, lack of mentorship, and work-life balance issues. One university implemented a program to support female faculty and students in STEM, offering mentorship, networking opportunities, and resources for career development. The program led to increased retention and advancement of women in STEM, demonstrating the effectiveness of targeted support and community-building efforts.

These case studies reveal common themes and lessons that can inform efforts to address gender dynamics in the workplace. First, intentional and sustained efforts are essential for promoting gender diversity and inclusion. Organizations must commit to creating equitable opportunities and addressing systemic barriers that hinder progress. Second, mentorship and support networks play a crucial role in empowering individuals to overcome challenges and achieve their goals. Providing access to mentors and allies can help individuals navigate complex dynamics and build confidence in their abilities.

Additionally, fostering open communication and understanding is key to addressing gender dynamics and enhancing collaboration. Encouraging dialogue about diverse perspectives and experiences can lead to more inclusive and innovative outcomes. Finally, recognizing and valuing diverse skills and contributions is essential for creating environments where all individuals feel respected and valued.

The insights gained from these case studies offer valuable perspectives on the complexities of gender dynamics at work and the potential for growth and transformation. By understanding the factors that influence gender dynamics and implementing strategies to address them, organizations can create more inclusive and equitable environments. These efforts remind us of the importance of ethical and responsible use of power, as well as the potential for empowerment and positive change.

Chapter 5

Media, Gender, and Power

Representation of Gender in Media

Harnessing the power of the wind has long been a dream for those seeking sustainable and renewable energy sources. Wind power, with its potential to reduce reliance on fossil fuels and decrease greenhouse gas emissions, offers a promising solution to the global energy crisis. However, like any energy source, wind power comes with its own set of benefits and challenges that must be carefully considered.

One of the most significant benefits of wind power is its environmental impact—or rather, the lack thereof. Unlike fossil fuels, wind energy is clean and produces no air or water pollution. This makes it an attractive option for reducing carbon footprints and combating climate change. Wind turbines generate electricity without emitting carbon dioxide or other harmful pollutants, contributing to cleaner air and a healthier planet. Additionally, wind power requires no water for cooling, unlike traditional power plants, which helps conserve valuable water resources.

Wind power is also a renewable resource, meaning it is inexhaustible and can be harnessed as long as the wind blows. This stands in stark contrast to finite fossil fuels, which are subject to depletion and price volatility. By investing in wind energy, countries can reduce their dependence on imported fuels and enhance their energy security. This not only stabilizes energy prices but also protects economies from the fluctuations of the global energy market.

The economic benefits of wind power extend beyond energy security. The wind energy sector has become a significant source of job creation, offering employment opportunities in manufacturing, installation, maintenance, and research and development. As the demand for wind energy grows, so too does the need for skilled workers, providing a boost to local economies and supporting community development. Moreover, wind farms can provide a steady income stream for landowners who lease their land for turbine installation, offering financial incentives for rural communities.

Despite these advantages, wind power faces several challenges that must be addressed to maximize its potential. One of the primary challenges is the variability of wind. Wind is an intermittent resource, meaning it does not blow consistently at all times. This variability can lead to fluctuations in energy production, making it difficult to rely solely on wind power for a stable energy supply. To mitigate this issue, wind energy is often integrated with other renewable sources, such as solar power, or supported by energy storage systems that can store excess energy for use during periods of low wind.

The siting of wind turbines presents another challenge. While wind farms can be located onshore or offshore, finding suitable sites that balance energy production with environmental and social considerations can be complex. Onshore wind farms may face opposition from local communities due to concerns about noise, visual impact, and effects on wildlife. Offshore wind farms, while less obtrusive to human populations, can be more expensive to build and maintain due to the harsh marine environment.

The impact of wind turbines on wildlife, particularly birds and bats, is a concern that has garnered significant attention. Collisions with turbine blades can pose a threat to these animals, leading to calls for careful site selection and the implementation of mitigation measures. Research and technological advancements are ongoing to develop solutions that minimize the impact on wildlife, such as radar systems that detect approaching birds and temporarily shut down turbines.

The initial cost of wind power infrastructure is another hurdle that must be overcome. While the cost of wind energy has decreased significantly over the past decade, the upfront investment required for turbine manufacturing, installation, and grid integration can be substantial. However, the long-term savings on fuel costs and the environmental benefits often outweigh these initial expenses. Governments and organizations can support the growth of wind energy by providing incentives, subsidies, and favorable policies that encourage investment and development.

Public perception and acceptance of wind power are crucial for its successful implementation. While many people support renewable energy in principle, they may have concerns about the impact of wind farms on their communities. Engaging with local stakeholders, providing transparent information, and addressing concerns through community consultations can help build trust and support for wind energy projects. By involving communities in the planning process and highlighting the benefits of wind power, such as job creation and environmental protection, developers can foster positive relationships and ensure the success of their projects.

The integration of wind power into existing energy grids presents technical challenges that require innovative solutions. The variability of wind energy necessitates the development of smart grid technologies that can efficiently manage and distribute electricity. These technologies include advanced forecasting systems, demand response programs, and energy storage solutions that enhance grid stability and reliability. By investing in grid modernization and infrastructure, countries can better accommodate the growing share of wind energy in their energy mix.

The insights gained from exploring the benefits and challenges of wind power offer valuable perspectives on the complexities of renewable energy and the potential for growth and transformation. By understanding the factors that influence wind energy development and implementing strategies to address them, we can work towards creating a more sustainable and resilient energy future. These efforts remind us of the importance of ethical and responsible use of energy resources, as well as the potential for empowerment and positive change.

Media Influence on Gender Norms

Media wields an undeniable influence over societal norms, shaping perceptions and expectations in ways both overt and subtle. Among the most profound impacts is the media's role in defining and perpetuating gender norms. These norms, which dictate the behaviors, roles, and attributes deemed appropriate for men and women, are often reinforced through various forms of media, including television, film, advertising, and digital platforms. Understanding how media influences gender norms is crucial for fostering a more equitable and inclusive society.

From a young age, individuals are exposed to media portrayals that shape their understanding of gender roles. Children's television shows and movies often feature characters that embody traditional gender stereotypes: boys are adventurous and strong, while girls are nurturing and passive. These early impressions can have a lasting impact, influencing children's self-perception and aspirations. For instance, a young girl who sees female characters primarily in caregiving roles may internalize the belief that her value lies in nurturing others, while a boy who sees male characters as heroes may feel pressured to conform to ideals of strength and bravery.

As individuals grow older, the media continues to play a significant role in reinforcing gender norms. Advertisements, in particular, are powerful vehicles for conveying messages about gender. They often depict men and women in stereotypical roles, with men portrayed as assertive and career-focused, and women as homemakers or objects of beauty. These portrayals not only reinforce existing stereotypes but also create unrealistic standards that individuals may feel compelled to meet. The pressure to conform to these ideals can lead to feelings of inadequacy and dissatisfaction, particularly when individuals do not see themselves reflected in the media they consume.

The impact of media on gender norms extends beyond individual perceptions to influence broader societal attitudes and behaviors. Media representations can shape public discourse and policy by framing certain issues in specific ways. For example, the portrayal of women in leadership roles in media can challenge traditional gender norms and inspire real-world change by normalizing the idea of women in positions of power. Conversely, the underrepresentation of women and minorities in media can perpetuate the status quo, reinforcing the notion that certain roles or industries are not accessible to all.

In recent years, there has been a growing recognition of the need for more diverse and accurate representations of gender in media. This shift is driven by advocacy from audiences, creators, and organizations who understand the power of media to shape cultural narratives. As a result, there has been an increase in media content that challenges traditional gender norms and offers more nuanced portrayals of individuals. Films and television shows are beginning to feature strong, complex female characters who defy stereotypes, as well as male characters who embrace vulnerability and emotional depth.

The rise of digital media and social platforms has also played a significant role in diversifying gender representation. These platforms provide a space for marginalized voices to share their stories and perspectives, challenging mainstream narratives and offering alternative representations of gender. Social media campaigns and movements, such as #MeToo and #TimesUp, have brought attention to issues of gender inequality and harassment, prompting conversations and actions that challenge the status quo.

Despite these positive developments, challenges remain in achieving truly equitable gender representation in media. The industry continues to grapple with issues of diversity and inclusion, both in front of and behind the camera. Women, particularly women of color, LGBTQ+ individuals, and those with disabilities, remain underrepresented in key creative and decision-making roles. This lack of diversity can result in media content that fails to accurately reflect the experiences and identities of all individuals.

To address these challenges, it is essential for media creators and organizations to prioritize diversity and inclusion in their work. This includes actively seeking out and amplifying underrepresented voices, both in storytelling and in leadership positions. By fostering an environment where diverse perspectives are valued and celebrated, the media industry can create content that resonates with a broader audience and reflects the richness of human experience.

Media literacy is another important tool for addressing gender representation. By equipping audiences with the skills to critically analyze media content, individuals can become more aware of the ways in which gender is portrayed and the impact of these portrayals. Media literacy education can empower individuals to question stereotypes, recognize bias, and advocate for more inclusive and accurate representations.

The role of consumers in shaping media representation should not be underestimated. Audiences have the power to influence the media landscape through their choices and voices. By supporting content that challenges traditional gender norms and promotes diversity, consumers can send a message to creators and organizations about the types of stories and representations they value. Engaging in conversations and advocacy around media representation can also contribute to a cultural shift towards greater inclusivity and equity.

The insights gained from examining media influence on gender norms offer valuable perspectives on the complexities of cultural narratives and the potential for growth and transformation. By understanding the factors that influence media portrayals and implementing strategies to address them, we can work towards creating a media landscape that reflects and celebrates the diversity of human experience. These efforts remind us of the importance of ethical and responsible storytelling, as well as the potential for empowerment and positive change.

The Role of Social Media in Gender Discourse

Social media has revolutionized the way we communicate, connect, and engage with the world around us. It has become a powerful platform for discourse, providing a space where individuals can share their thoughts, experiences, and perspectives on a wide range of topics, including gender. The role of social media in gender discourse is multifaceted, offering both opportunities and challenges in the pursuit of gender equality and understanding.

One of the most significant contributions of social media to gender discourse is its ability to amplify marginalized voices. Historically, traditional media has often overlooked or misrepresented the experiences of women, LGBTQ+ individuals, and other marginalized groups. Social media platforms, however, provide an accessible and democratic space where these voices can be heard and shared widely. This has led to the emergence of grassroots movements and campaigns that challenge existing gender norms and advocate for change. Hashtags like #MeToo, #BlackLivesMatter, and #TimesUp have gained global traction, highlighting issues of gender-based violence, racial injustice, and workplace discrimination. These movements have sparked important conversations and brought attention to systemic inequalities that might otherwise have remained hidden.

Social media also facilitates the sharing of personal stories and experiences, creating a sense of community and solidarity among individuals who may feel isolated or marginalized. By connecting with others who share similar experiences, individuals can find support, validation, and empowerment. This sense of community is particularly important for those who may not have access to supportive networks in their offline lives. For example, LGBTQ+ individuals in conservative or hostile environments can find acceptance and understanding through online communities, helping them navigate the challenges they face.

The interactive nature of social media allows for real-time engagement and dialogue, enabling users to participate in discussions and debates about gender issues. This immediacy fosters a dynamic exchange of ideas and perspectives, encouraging critical thinking and reflection. Social media users can challenge stereotypes, question assumptions, and propose alternative narratives, contributing to a more nuanced and inclusive understanding of gender. This participatory aspect of social media democratizes the discourse, allowing individuals from diverse backgrounds to contribute to the conversation and influence public opinion.

However, the role of social media in gender discourse is not without its challenges. The same platforms that amplify marginalized voices can also be used to spread misinformation, perpetuate stereotypes, and incite harassment. Online spaces can become battlegrounds where toxic behavior and hostility thrive, particularly towards those who challenge traditional gender norms. Women, LGBTQ+ individuals, and other marginalized groups often face targeted harassment and abuse, which can have serious psychological and emotional impacts. This hostile environment can deter individuals from participating in online discourse, limiting the diversity of voices and perspectives.

The anonymity afforded by social media can exacerbate these issues, as individuals may feel emboldened to engage in harmful behavior without fear of consequences. This anonymity can also make it difficult to hold individuals accountable for their actions, allowing harmful narratives and behaviors to persist. Addressing these challenges requires a concerted effort from social media platforms, users, and policymakers to create safer and more inclusive online spaces. Implementing robust moderation policies, providing resources for users facing harassment, and promoting digital literacy are essential steps in fostering a more positive and productive discourse.

Despite these challenges, social media remains a valuable tool for advancing gender discourse and promoting social change. By leveraging the power of social media, individuals and organizations can raise awareness, mobilize support, and advocate for policy changes that promote gender equality. Social media campaigns can reach a global audience, transcending geographical and cultural boundaries to unite individuals in a common cause. This global reach allows for the sharing of diverse perspectives and experiences, enriching the discourse and fostering a more comprehensive understanding of gender issues.

The role of influencers and public figures on social media also plays a significant part in shaping gender discourse. Influencers with large followings have the power to sway public opinion and bring attention to important issues. By using their platforms to advocate for gender equality and challenge stereotypes, influencers can inspire their audiences to engage with these topics and take action. However, the influence of public figures can be a double-edged sword, as their messages may not always align with the goals of gender equality. It is important for audiences to critically evaluate the content they consume and consider the motivations and perspectives of those they follow.

Social media's role in gender discourse is further complicated by the algorithms that govern what content users see. These algorithms are designed to prioritize content that generates engagement, which can lead to the amplification of sensational or polarizing content. This can create echo chambers where users are exposed to a narrow range of perspectives, reinforcing existing beliefs and limiting exposure to diverse viewpoints. To counteract this, users can actively seek out diverse voices and engage with content that challenges their assumptions, fostering a more balanced and informed discourse.

The insights gained from examining the role of social media in gender discourse offer valuable perspectives on the complexities of digital communication and the potential for growth and transformation. By understanding the factors that influence online discourse and implementing strategies to address them, we can work towards creating a more inclusive and equitable digital landscape. These efforts remind us of the importance of ethical and responsible use of digital platforms, as well as the potential for empowerment and positive change.

Power Dynamics in Media Industries

Power dynamics within media industries are a complex web of influence, control, and negotiation that shape the content we consume and the narratives that dominate public discourse. These dynamics are influenced by a variety of factors, including ownership structures, regulatory environments, and cultural contexts. Understanding these power dynamics is essential for anyone seeking to navigate or reform the media landscape.

At the heart of media power dynamics lies the issue of ownership. A small number of conglomerates often control a significant portion of media outlets, leading to a concentration of power that can influence the diversity and objectivity of content. These conglomerates, driven by profit motives, may prioritize content that appeals to the broadest audience or aligns with their corporate interests, potentially sidelining alternative or dissenting voices. This concentration of ownership can lead to a homogenization of media content, where diverse perspectives and stories are underrepresented.

The influence of advertisers further complicates the power dynamics within media industries. Advertising revenue is a primary source of income for many media outlets, creating a dependency that can affect editorial decisions. Media organizations may be reluctant to publish content that could alienate advertisers or challenge their interests, leading to self-censorship or biased reporting. This relationship between media and advertisers underscores the importance of maintaining editorial independence to ensure that content remains objective and diverse.

Regulatory environments also play a crucial role in shaping power dynamics within media industries. Governments and regulatory bodies can influence media content through legislation, licensing, and censorship. In some cases, media outlets may face pressure to align with government narratives or face repercussions, such as fines or revocation of licenses. This can lead to a media landscape where certain viewpoints are privileged over others, limiting the diversity of perspectives available to the public.

Cultural contexts and societal norms further influence power dynamics within media industries. Media content is often shaped by the cultural values and expectations of the society in which it is produced. This can lead to the reinforcement of dominant cultural narratives and the marginalization of minority voices. For example, media industries in patriarchal societies may perpetuate gender stereotypes and limit the representation of women and LGBTQ+ individuals. Challenging these cultural norms requires a concerted effort to promote diversity and inclusion within media content and production.

The role of gatekeepers within media industries is another critical aspect of power dynamics. Editors, producers, and executives often serve as gatekeepers, deciding which stories are told and how they are presented. These individuals wield significant influence over the media landscape, shaping public discourse and determining which issues receive attention. The decisions made by gatekeepers can reflect their own biases and priorities, further influencing the diversity and objectivity of media content.

The rise of digital media and social platforms has introduced new dynamics into the media landscape, challenging traditional power structures. These platforms provide individuals with the ability to create and share content independently, bypassing traditional gatekeepers and reaching global audiences. This democratization of content creation has led to a proliferation of diverse voices and perspectives, challenging the dominance of established media outlets. However, digital platforms also present their own set of power dynamics, with algorithms and platform policies influencing the visibility and reach of content.

The role of algorithms in shaping media content is a significant aspect of power dynamics in the digital age. Algorithms determine what content users see based on their preferences and behaviors, creating personalized media experiences. While this can enhance user engagement, it can also lead to the creation of echo chambers, where users are exposed to a narrow range of perspectives that reinforce their existing beliefs. This can limit the diversity of content and contribute to the polarization of public discourse.

The influence of social media influencers and content creators further complicates power dynamics within media industries. Influencers with large followings can shape public opinion and drive trends, wielding significant power over their audiences. This influence can be both positive and negative, as influencers can promote diverse perspectives and challenge dominant narratives, but they can also spread misinformation or reinforce harmful stereotypes. The power of influencers highlights the importance of media literacy and critical thinking in navigating the media landscape.

Addressing power dynamics within media industries requires a multifaceted approach that promotes diversity, inclusion, and accountability. Media organizations can prioritize diversity in hiring and content production, ensuring that a range of voices and perspectives are represented. This includes amplifying marginalized voices and challenging dominant narratives that perpetuate inequality. Regulatory bodies can support these efforts by promoting policies that encourage diversity and protect editorial independence.

Media literacy education is another essential tool for addressing power dynamics within media industries. By equipping individuals with the skills to critically analyze media content, audiences can become more aware of the factors that influence media narratives and the impact of power dynamics. Media literacy empowers individuals to question biases, recognize manipulation, and seek out diverse perspectives, fostering a more informed and engaged public.

The role of consumers in shaping power dynamics within media industries should not be underestimated. Audiences have the power to influence media content through their choices and voices. By supporting diverse and independent media outlets, consumers can send a message to media organizations about the types of content they value. Engaging in conversations and advocacy around media representation and accountability can also contribute to a cultural shift towards greater inclusivity and equity.

The insights gained from examining power dynamics within media industries offer valuable perspectives on the complexities of media production and the potential for growth and transformation. By understanding the factors that influence media content and implementing strategies to address them, we can work towards creating a media landscape that reflects and celebrates the diversity of human experience. These efforts remind us of the importance of ethical and responsible storytelling, as well as the potential for empowerment and positive change.

Changing Narratives and Future Trends

Narratives shape our understanding of the world, influencing perceptions, behaviors, and societal norms. As society evolves, so too do the narratives that define it. In recent years, there has been a significant shift in the stories we tell and the ways we tell them, driven by cultural, technological, and social changes. These changing narratives are not only reflective of current realities but also indicative of future trends that will shape our world.

One of the most profound shifts in narrative has been the move towards inclusivity and diversity.

Historically, dominant narratives have often marginalized or excluded certain voices, particularly those of women, people of color, LGBTQ+ individuals, and other underrepresented groups. However, there is a growing recognition of the importance of diverse perspectives in enriching our understanding of the world. This shift is evident in various forms of media, from literature and film to advertising and journalism, where stories that celebrate diversity and challenge stereotypes are increasingly gaining prominence.

The rise of digital media has played a crucial role in facilitating this shift. Social media platforms, blogs, and independent publishing have democratized storytelling, allowing individuals from diverse backgrounds to share their experiences and perspectives with a global audience. This has led to the emergence of new voices and narratives that challenge traditional power structures and offer alternative viewpoints. As a result, audiences are exposed to a broader range of stories that reflect the complexity and richness of human experience.

In addition to promoting diversity, changing narratives are also characterized by a focus on authenticity and transparency. In an era of information overload and digital manipulation, audiences are increasingly seeking genuine and honest stories that resonate with their own experiences. This demand for authenticity is driving a shift away from polished, idealized narratives towards more raw and relatable storytelling. Brands, media outlets, and content creators are responding by prioritizing transparency and honesty in their messaging, fostering trust and connection with their audiences.

The changing narratives are also influenced by technological advancements that are transforming the way stories are created and consumed. Virtual reality, augmented reality, and interactive media are pushing the boundaries of traditional storytelling, offering immersive and engaging experiences that captivate audiences. These technologies allow for more dynamic and participatory narratives, where audiences can become active participants in the story rather than passive observers. This shift towards interactive storytelling is opening up new possibilities for creativity and innovation, challenging creators to think beyond conventional formats.

As narratives evolve, so too do the themes and topics that dominate them. Environmental sustainability, social justice, and mental health are increasingly becoming central themes in contemporary storytelling. These topics reflect the pressing issues of our time and resonate with audiences who are seeking stories that address the challenges and opportunities of the modern world. By engaging with these themes, narratives have the power to inspire action, raise awareness, and drive social change.

The changing narratives are also indicative of broader cultural and societal shifts. As traditional norms and values are questioned and redefined, narratives are evolving to reflect these changes. For example, the concept of success is being reimagined, moving away from material wealth and status towards personal fulfillment and well-being. Similarly, narratives around gender and identity are becoming more fluid and inclusive, challenging binary notions and embracing a spectrum of experiences.

Looking to the future, several trends are likely to shape the narratives of tomorrow. The continued rise of digital media and technology will further democratize storytelling, enabling even more voices to be heard. As audiences become more discerning and demand greater authenticity, narratives will need to prioritize honesty and transparency to maintain relevance and trust. Additionally, the growing emphasis on diversity and inclusivity will continue to drive the creation of stories that reflect the full spectrum of human experience.

The integration of artificial intelligence and machine learning into storytelling is another trend that holds significant potential. These technologies can analyze vast amounts of data to identify patterns and insights, informing the creation of narratives that resonate with audiences on a deeper level. While the use of AI in storytelling raises ethical considerations, it also presents opportunities for innovation and personalization, allowing for more tailored and engaging narratives.

The changing narratives and future trends offer valuable insights into the evolving landscape of storytelling. By embracing diversity, authenticity, and innovation, narratives have the power to shape perceptions, challenge norms, and inspire change. As we navigate this dynamic landscape, it is essential to remain open to new possibilities and perspectives, recognizing the potential of storytelling to connect, inform, and transform.